I SHALL BE COOL

Linda Spencer

Linda was born in Easington Colliery, Co Durham in 1958, she then moved to Leicester in the early 1960's, which is where she spent her childhood. But, it was in 'Shakespeare County,' Warwickshire, where she says she 'grew up' during and after completing her counselling diploma.

She is now an experienced counsellor, supervisor, & trainer, and a behavioural family therapist. She has three grown up children and nine grandchildren.

Linda is also an author of self help books, children's books, counseling text books and novels.

Holding on to anger feeds upon itself

Unresolved anger is a virus

That needs not even air

To propagate contagion

Whenever it is shared.

The anger can't be placed in quarantine

To contain its vicious spread

For anger feeds upon itself

And burns a flaming red.

Anger is all consuming

Anger does not desist

From destroying sensibilities

In that haze of its red mist.

David Keig
Adapted

I shall be cool

Chapters

Prologue

Chapter One: What is anger?

Chapter Two: Anger signs and symptoms

Chapter Three: What makes you angry and why?

Chapter Four: Managing your anger healthily?

Chapter Five: The umbrella of anger

Chapter Six: Using CBT to manage your anger.

Chapter Seven: Transactional Analysis and anger.

Chapter Eight: Letting go of historical anger.

Chapter Nine: Stress and anger

Chapter Ten: Anger Management and Techniques

Epilogue

Prologue

This is my fifth book in the "I shall be….." self help range. My other books are as follows:

- I shall wear purple – Emotional growth
- I shall be clean – Substance misuse
- I shall be blue - Depression
- I shall be calm - Anxiety

I hope that you enjoy this book as much as the others, and that it helps clients and therapists when working with anger.

Anger is something that we all experience during our life many times. The question is often asked are we born with the feeling of anger – nature or nurture.   We are all aware of the babies cry when they are hungry who isn't fed straight away. Is that anger or hunger?

Many theorists will say that a true temper tantrum doesn't start until a baby is between twelve and eighteen months old.

According to Yale Medicine Child Study Centre clinical psychologist Dennis Sukhodolsky, it's not unusual for a child younger than four to have as many as nine tantrums a week, with episodes of crying, kicking, stomping, hitting and pushing, that last five to ten minutes. (Dennis Sukhodolsky, n.d.)

So, although we may be born with the ability to feel anger and frustration if our nappy needs changing or we are hungry, it is believed that anger styles are learned behaviours. We all experience anger in response to frustrating or abusive situations; however it is how we respond to these that is learned.

We learn how to manage our anger by firstly watching how the people around us respond to anger, such as our caregivers. If we see Dad or Mum or other family members lashing out in anger, verbally or physically this results in us maybe growing up to believe that this is the normal way to express their anger.

Likewise, if a child is rewarded for being a bully, or fighting back in their frustrations this can create a pattern of this sort of behaviour. Equally, if a child is punished for expressing a feeling of anger, this can lead to them learning to suppress their anger which is equally unhealthy, as this leads to a 'bottling up' of our anger which will inevitably result in periodic angry outbursts.

How anger manifests in our life by outbursts or suppression of anger, what is true of us all is that we all experience feelings of anger and so therefore this book can be helpful for most people.

I sometimes hear people say "I don't get angry," of course we all 'get angry.' It is a normal human emotion, what they may mean is I don't express anger, which can be just as debilitating as someone who expresses it aggressively or violently.

I have noticed during my work that some people express their anger outwardly, whereas others express it inwardly. Both will experience psychological problems during their lifetimes.

A lot of our problems in life in our relationships are because of the way in which we express our anger.

This book helps you to learn to express your normal emotion of anger in a healthy and constructive way. It contains notes for therapists, exercises and anger management worksheets.

This book is, as is all my others, a tool to help clients and therapists alike in working with anger and learning constructive ways in which they can manage their anger.

This sign represents note for therapists

This sign is for anger management exercises to try

This sign is for anger worksheets

The goal is not to ever feel angry

The goal is to understand your anger and to choose healthy ways to respond to it.

Chapter One
What is anger?

A nger is a feeling. It is not a forbidden feeling, nor a feeling that you should suppress. Anger is not the same as 'losing your temper', nor is it the same as 'violence'.

Losing your temper is destructive. It is to do with an outburst which is the outcome of frustration and helplessness.

VIOLENCE is an outburst of accumulated unused energy. It is being out of control. It makes problems worse or creates extra ones!

Many of us are taught that 'violence' and 'loss of temper' is wrong, which is correct. The trouble is that we confuse these two with 'anger', so we also come to believe that 'anger' too is wrong and should be avoided. This we learn at a very early age.

Imagine that you are two years old and you are angry because Mum has put milk in your bottle and you wanted orange juice.

Or your big sister is playing with your favourite toy and won't let you have it. We don't have the resources at two to say,

"Hey Mom, I'm angry with you right now as you have given me milk instead of orange. Can you change it please?" or,

"Please can I play with that toy when you are finished with it" to your big sister.

So, you throw the bottle across the room, the lid comes off and milk explodes all over Mums new sofa. Whoops! Gee, Mum's mad and gives you a big telling off or in some households a smack on the backside. Or you snatch the toy off your sister, she cries and you are put on the naughty step.

We soon learn that ***"It is not okay to be angry around here"*** so we grow up believing that 'anger' is a forbidden feeling. (However, we have actually got into trouble for the acts of violence or loss of temper – not our anger).

We are not able to differentiate at that age the difference between anger and violence. Many of us are not taught that we are on the *'naughty step'* because of our aggressive behaviour not because we are angry. We are not always taught that it is okay to feel angry, it is a normal feeling.

We then begin to suppress our anger, which can subsequently lead to a loss of temper or violence, usually someone at sometime gets the whole lot of our 'built up' anger. This then leaves people feeling confused because the anger is too big for the actual 'crime.'

Anger is an emotional state that may range from minor irritation to intense rage. The physical effects of anger include increased heart rate and blood pressure. People that are intensely angry may go red in the face and stomp about.

Clients may act their anger out in the therapy room, it is important that if you feel angry at their behaviour that you do not act out your anger. Recognise that this is a process and unless you are at risk of harm it is about staying with that process.

It gives you an indication of how the client behaves when angry and how this might impact on others and may be indicative of why they have the interpersonal difficulties they have.

Stay calm, keep your voice calm and feedback to the client that you can see they are very angry and would like to help them to process this anger. Invite them to sit down and take some deep breathes before they explain to you what their anger is about. You may say "I am struggling to understand or hear what you are saying so that I can help you. It would be helpful if you could sit down and tell me as calmly as you can what is going on for you."

Anger can manifest itself in a number of different ways, not all anger is expressed in the same way. Anger and aggression can be outward, inward or passive.

Outward, involves expressing your anger and aggression in an obvious way. Such as shouting, cursing, throwing or breaking things, or being verbally or physically abusive towards others.

Inward, is directed at yourself. It involves negative self talk, denying yourself things that make you happy or even basic needs, such as food. Self harm and isolating yourself from people are other ways anger can be directed inward.

Passive, this involves using subtle and indirect ways to express anger, such as giving someone the silent treatment, sulking, being sarcastic and making snide remarks.

Getting this book you may have recognised that you have some anger issues. You may have anger issues if:

- You feel angry often
- Your anger is impacting on your relationships
- You feel that your anger seems out of control
- Your anger is hurting self and/or others
- Your anger causes you to say or do things you regret
- You are verbally or physically abusive

If you believe your anger is out of control or if it is negatively affecting your life or relationships, consider seeking help from a mental health professional, who can help determine if you have an underlying mental health condition that is causing your anger issues and requires treatment.

A mental health professional can also help you to work through your anger and identify any underlying issues that may be a contributing factor. With anger management and other treatments, and maybe with the help of this book, you can get your anger under control.

Anger can be caused by both external and internal events. You could be angry at a specific person (Such as a friend a partner or a child) or an event (a traffic jam, someone pushing in the queue), or your anger could be caused by worrying about your personal problems.

Anger is a natural response to threats which often evokes aggressive feelings and behaviours, which allow us to fight and to defend ourselves when we are attacked. A certain amount of anger, therefore, is necessary to our survival.

Although we need some level of anger to survive, we can't physically lash out at every person or object that irritates or annoys us; laws, social norms, and common sense place limits on how far our anger can take us.

Anger is a natural feeling, experienced when people feel frustrated, hurt, rejected or hostile. It's a powerful emotion, and unless it's managed properly, it can have a devastating effect on the family, your work and your overall wellbeing.

We often get messages to 'be positive' and to let go of our anger and to teach ourselves never to feel angry. The reality is that we are all going to feel angry sometimes. Equally, when we feel angry we can often feel guilty for feeling this way. It is okay to feel angry and being able to feel this emotion is a healthy thing for you to do.

Emotions like sadness, guilt, fear, envy and anger are an important part of your emotional intelligence and emotional growth. They are just as important as feeling joy, happiness, contentment and love.

It is important therefore that you do not deny feelings that you consider to be negative or feel that you should not express negative emotions. They are just as important as your positive emotions. This book will teach you:

- ✓ To be aware when you are feeling angry
- ✓ Take the time to understand your anger
- ✓ Finally to choose healthy ways to respond

Helping clients to identify what may be causing their anger is often the first step in learning how to better deal with their anger.

A moment of patience, in a moment of anger saves you a hundred moments of regret.

Chapter Two
Anger signs and symptoms

Anger feels different for everyone. You may experience some of the following. You might have other experiences or difficulties that aren't listed here. We will firstly look at the effects that anger may have on your body:

- A churning feeling in your stomach
- A tightness in your chest
- An feeling of tension in your muscles
- Legs going weak
- Sweating (especially your palms)
- An increased and rapid heartbeat
- Pins and needles in your limbs
- Feeling hot
- An urge to go to the toilet
- Headache

- Dizziness
- Shaking or trembling
- Feeling that you want to cry
- Tightness of the throat
- Change in breathing

EXERCISE

Write down any bodily reactions which you have when you are feeling angry.

Now let's look at the effects that anger has on your emotions:

- Tense, nervous and unable to relax
- Feeling resentful towards other people or situations
- Feeling irritated
- Feeling a red mist
- Feeling guilty
- Feeling shame
- Feeing attacked
- Feeling humiliated

EXERCISE

Write down any bodily reactions which you have when feeling angry.

Are there any thoughts that you have that make you angry? Here are a few that you may have:

- "Nobody likes me"
- "S/he is scamming me"
- "S/he is a liar"
- "S/he is taking the Mickey out of me"
- "S/he is avoiding me"
- "S/he has done this all wrong"
- "I am hopeless"
- "I can't do anything right"
- "I should have known better"
- "They are leaving me out"
- "They are laughing at me"

Write down any thoughts that may trigger your anger.

When you are able to recognise the signs it will help you to think about how you want to react to the situation. It will enable you to rationalise any irrational thoughts or calm down some of your feelings. It will give you a chance to 'breathe'.

This can be difficult in the heat of the moment, but the earlier that you notice how you are thinking, feeling physically and emotionally you are asking yourself what painful emotion you are feeling in this situation when you became angry.

It allows you to have a bit of compassion for your own pain and often stops you from taking that pain out on others. Nurturing your own pain calms you down almost immediately.

Equally, it may not be anger that you are really feeling, it may be sadness or unresolved pain from the past. You may be putting someone else's head from the past on to the shoulders of someone in the here and now. The anger may not actually belong to them. You may have been storing this anger up, to then dump they whole shebang on this new person, a person who does not deserve that intensity of anger or any at all.

There is a lot to be said for the old saying *"count to ten."*

Anger is a very energising and motivating emotion. It's a natural and normal response to feeling threatened, or thinking something is unjust, unfair. Sometimes we're right to think and respond in that way.

It can be a very appropriate and healthy response.

For instance, we see a crime being committed, someone being attacked, we might instinctively react and rush to help the person being attacked, and stop the attacker. However, there are times when, perhaps due to our past experiences, something around us, a noise, the way someone looks at us, the way someone says something, a gesture – anything – triggers this response.

We can misinterpret situations and believe others are having a go at us, that we're being criticised or attacked in some way, which then starts the angry cycle.

We can get into the habit of responding this way, and it can be a hard habit to shake. This vicious cycle though, is a cycle – and we can break cycles, particularly at the points where we think and act, we can learn to think and act differently.   We all have the ability to change the way we respond when we are angry.   We all have the ability to step off this cycle of anger, if we choose to.

ALERT: On guard

We can learn to monitor our own anger, what makes us angry, what are our triggers. We can get in touch with our body when we feel angry and learn to be aware of our 'symptoms' and turn down the sensitivity setting to process before acting out.

THOUGHTS

We can learn to monitor our thoughts and reality test those thoughts such as:

- ☐ "It's unfair"
- ☐ "I am being badly treated"
- ☐ "I'm under attack"
- ☐ "They're having a go at me"

EMOTIONS

We can learn to understand our own emotions and the difference between anger, rage, frustration, irritation and or anxiety, guilt or shame.

PHYSICAL AROUSAL

We can learn to recognise our body's alarm system such as adrenaline which energises and motivates our bodies, providing a physical urge and readiness to deal with a situation in a physical way. This is a normal fight or flight response. It is an automatic response when we believe we are being threatened, criticised or attacked although this may not always be a reality. We may need to do something to calm these feelings down. When they are physical we may need to do something physical to release them. That does not mean 'a fight' – a run, a dance, exercise of any nature can do this.

However, We may respond to this surge of adrenalin by raising our voice, sarcasm, shout, scream, confront, stamp feet, clench fists, lash out, violence, fight, harm others or self or drink or use drugs to manage these feelings. All of which will create further problems in our life.

The adrenaline is there for us to face and deal with real danger, however often our mind will trick us with imagined danger and our bodies will react in the same way as if it was real.

On the following page there is a worksheet for you to explore the reactions you may experience in your body when feeling angry. Try colouring in the ones that apply to you and add some ones of your own too.

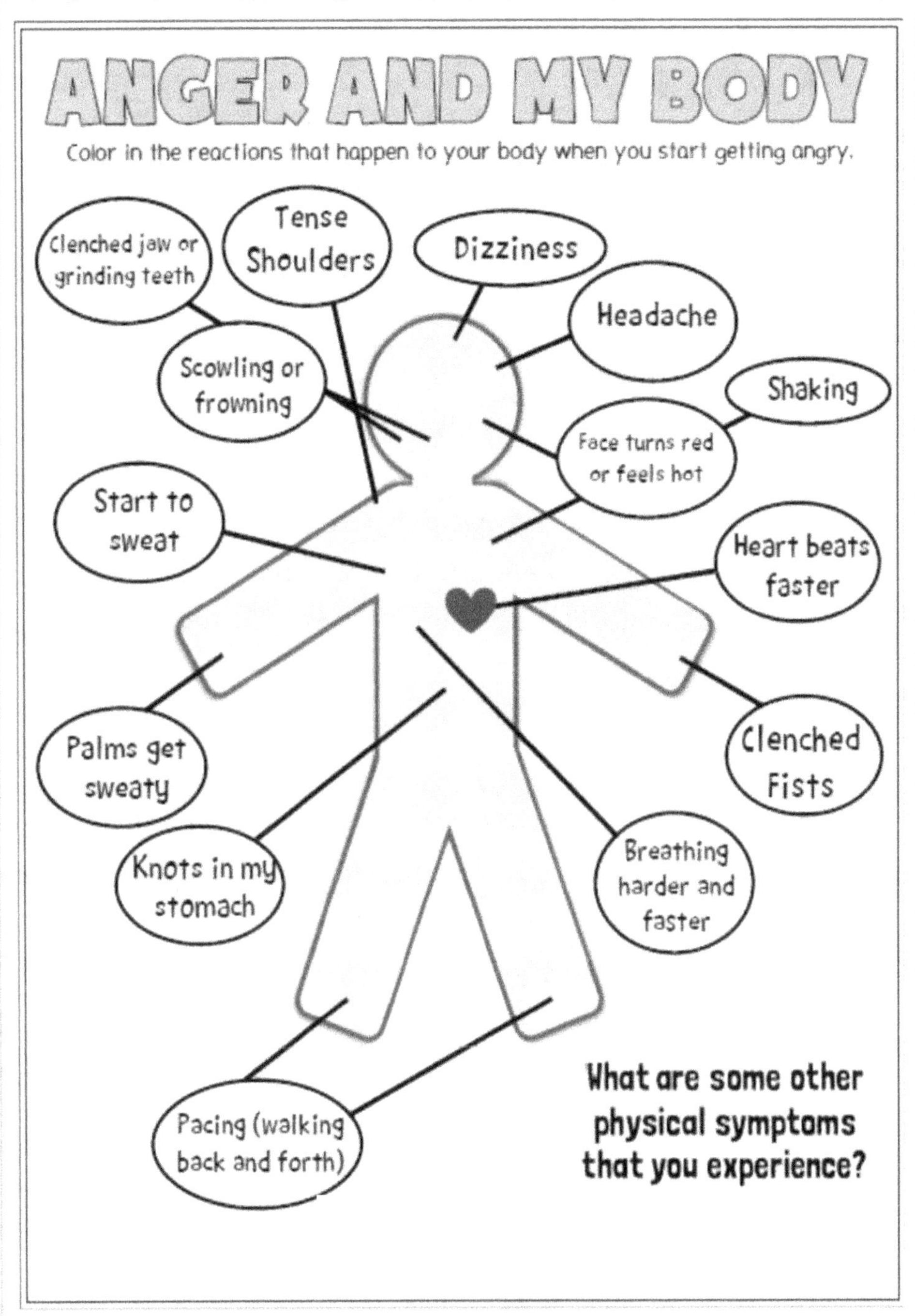

ANGER AND MY BODY
Color in the reactions that happen to your body when you start getting angry.
Clenched jaw or grinding teeth
Tense Shoulders
Dizziness
Headache
Scowling or frowning
Shaking
Face turns red or feels hot
Start to sweat
Heart beats faster
Palms get sweaty
Clenched Fists
Knots in my stomach
Breathing harder and faster
Pacing (walking back and forth)
What are some other physical symptoms that you experience?

Reasons why it is okay to be angry:

It keeps you safe. To be able to feel anger is a necessary skill. It gives you the ability to be aware of a situation that is abusive or neglectful. If you are unable to feel your anger it may hide the fact that you are in an abusive relationship and unable to protest about the way in which you are being treated.

It motivates you to take action. Feeling angry can motivate you to take action and make positive changes in your life.

Help you to access deeper emotions. Anger is often the first sign that something is wrong. It can help you to explore unconscious feelings that are a trigger for your anger. It can help you to process painful feelings from the past. It can help you to get to the root of problems.

It can help you to decide what you want. Anger can help you to explore what it is that you really want, and get you out of a rut.

It can improve your relationships. People who hide their true feelings are often seen as phony to others. Being happy all the time is not natural. It can make those that feel and express their anger feel inadequate because you do not feel or express anger and are always happy. It is not being real and when you are not real it depletes you of the ability to have an intimate relationship with others.

It can prevent you from carrying around unresolved feelings. If you feel and express your anger then the weight of unresolved anger will not fester and hang around your neck dragging you and sometimes others down.

It can make you happy. You cannot have more than one emotion at the same time. Feeling angry all the time denies you of the nice feelings such as happiness and joy.

It helps you to understand and not be scared of other people's feelings. If you cannot accept your own feelings then you will struggle to accept and understand other people's feelings.

Like all things when you have too much of something it can make you feel unwell, even sick. The same applies to 'anger'. Too much anger can:

- Destroy relationships
- Get us into conflict, verbal and physical with others
- Cause us to be judgemental
- Make us intolerant of others
- React in an out of proportion manner to situations
- Compromise our immune system, which leads us to lengthy bouts of illness
- Give us banging headaches

It really is not worth feeling angry for too long. Don't you agree?

Anybody can become angry that is easy, but to become angry with the right person, to the right degree, at the right time, for the right purpose and in the right way is not always what we do, but is the healthiest way to manage your anger.

Chapter Three
What makes you angry and why?

Feelings of anger can be like a pot of boiling water on the stove. First the water starts off at a slow simmer with gentle bubbles creating a little heat and steam. If not dealt with at this point, the temperature builds, the water becomes hotter. If still not dealt with it reaches boiling point, this is when it becomes overwhelmingly powerful, even dangerous as it becomes scalding.

If the boiling continues, the water disappears and you are left with an empty pot which is burnt and foul smelling. This is the burnt feeling that you may feel inside, when you have expressed your feeling in a destructive way.

Anger, too, can simmer, intensify and boil over if you try to keep it covered up. Concealed or covered up anger can eventually leave you feeling empty, burned out and unable to accomplish anything.

Holding on to anger is like holding on to a hot piece of coal, the only one to get burned is you!

Anger can arise for many reasons and are often unique to you and what annoys you. For example one person may become very angry at being told a lie, for another it may not even raise their temperature, let alone their anger.

It can also be how we interpret and react to certain situations. We all have our own triggers for what makes us angry. Some examples may be:

- When we feel threatened or attacked
- When we feel frustrated or powerless
- When we feel invalidated
- When we feel treated unfairly
- When people are not respecting our feelings or possessions
- When we feel out of control

How you interpret and react to a situation can depend on lots of factors in your life including:

Your childhood and upbringing

We may get messages as children such as 'you need to be in control of every situation,' 'Make sure you are never treated unfairly,' 'Be tough with everyone.' So when any of these things happen in our adult life we feel angry.

We may have suppressed anger as a child, perhaps when we were out of control or treated unfairly and so when we experience these behaviours towards us as adults it resurrects those feelings from our past. We have a double whammy of anger.

How we learn to cope with angry feelings is often influenced by our upbringing. We are given messages about anger as children that make it harder to manage as an adult.

You may have grown up thinking that it is always okay to act out your anger aggressively or violently. This message may have been verbalised to you or more covertly expressed in the way that we see others act out their anger. If this happened then you may not have learned how to understand and manage your angry feelings.

This could mean that you have angry outbursts either verbally or physically whenever you don't like the way someone is behaving or when you are in a situation you don't like.

Or, you may have been brought up to believe that you should not complain or express your anger. Again this could have been communicated to you verbally or non-verbally. You may have been punished for expressing your anger as a child.

This could mean that you tend to suppress your anger and it becomes a long term problem, where you react inappropriately to new situations you are not comfortable with.

Some people who suppress their anger have a monthly outburst on people which mean that the person is getting a build up of anger for a lot of people, which is undeserved.

Some people who suppress their anger might also turn this inwards on to themselves. They may do this by self harm or negative self talk.

You may have witnessed your parents or other adult's anger when it is out of control and learned to think of anger as something which is destructive and terrifying.

This could mean that you now feel afraid of your own anger and therefore do not feel safe in expressing your feelings when something or someone does something that angers you. These feelings might then surface at another unconnected time, which may feel hard to explain.

Or seeing significant others violence in your life as a child might teach you to be aggressive and violent yourself as an adult.

Past experiences

If you have experienced situations in the past that made you feel angry, such as abuse, trauma, bullying etc and you were not able to express your anger safely then you may be still coping with those angry feelings now. If this is the case, whenever you re-experience similar real or imagined situations in the now it may raise the anger that you felt in the past.

This would mean that you find certain situations particularly challenging.   To manage your anger effectively you need to be aware of the situations linked to the past that may trigger you anger in the current situation.

EXERCISE

Think about any past triggers that may impact on the present.

It is important when learning how to manage your anger that you are mindful that your present feelings of anger may not only be about the current situation but may also be related to the past experience, which can mean that the anger you are feeling in the present is at a level that reflects your past situation. This may be why you feel so overwhelmed in anger.

When we become aware of all our conscious and unconscious triggers it can help us to find ways of responding to situations in the present in a safer and less distressed way.

The past is history, the future a mystery, so enjoy the present because it is a gift.

Current circumstances

If you are dealing with a lot of other problems in your life at the moment, you might find yourself feeling angry more easily than usual, or getting angry at unrelated things.

What is also important to remember is that anger can also be part of grief. I have seen a lot of grieving people express displaced anger on to innocent people. This can all be on a unconscious level, you may not be consciously aware that your anger is related to loss.

When we lose someone important to us, it can be very difficult to cope with all the conflicting emotions. Counselling may help you to process and separate out your feelings and normalise them with you.

There may be times, also when you are in a situation that makes you feel angry but, you don't feel able to express that anger directly at the person or resolve it. You may then find that you dump that anger on a different person, someone in the shopping queue for example or another driver on the road.

EXERCISE

If you are starting to feel angry whilst reading this book, be mindful that this is not unusual as you are thinking about past anger and things that anger you.

So, *'breathe'* – stopping for a breath allows you to take a moment to concentrate on your breathing and not your anger. It gives you something else to focus on.

Remember

TO BE ANGRY IS OKAY!
IT IS A NORMAL FEELING TO BE EXPRESSED
TO LOSE YOUR TEMPER OR BE VIOLENT IS NOT OKAY!
IT IS A LOSS OF CONTROL AND LEAVES US POWERLESS

One way in which we learn to suppress our anger and release them in a loss of temper or in some cases violence is, what ERIC BERNE the founder of a psychotherapy model called 'Transactional Analysis' describes as "collecting trading stamps". He says that we collect stamps which are resentments that we suppress and store and then cash them in on others after a period of time.

For example: If you can imagine that you come into work each night and.....................

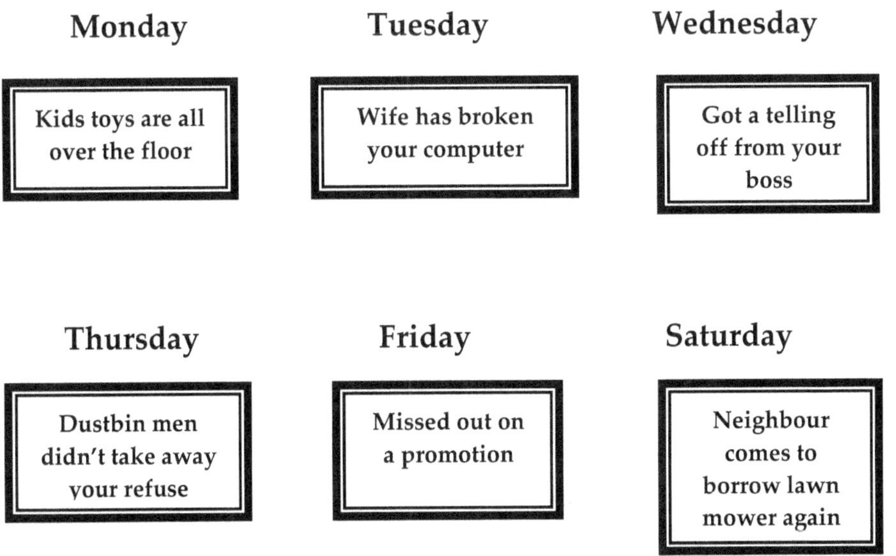

The neighbour gets the………………..

YOUR NEIGHBOUR HAS GOT YOUR WEEKLY COLLECTION OF TRADING STAMPS!

Eric Berne says that once enough stamps are stored, we find a way to cash them in, on the excuse that we have earned the right to a free outburst! The way to deal with our anger is to express each feeling of anger in the here and now.

Whether you anger is about something that happened in the past or is something that is going on in the present, thinking about how and why we interpret and react to situations can help us to learn new ways of expressing our anger and learn how to cope with our emotions better.

On the following pages is an 'Anger diary' to help you to monitor and explore your own anger. It may help you to learn how to *catch* your anger before it takes over.

ANGER DIARY

Example

TRIGGER	My husband left motorbike oil all over my carpet. I have asked him so many times to take his shoes off at the door.
WARNING SIGN	At the start of my anger I noticed my hands shaking, then the more I thought about it my face went red and heart beat fast.
ANGER RESPONSE	I yelled at my husband and called him horrible names. I could myself getting madder and madder
OUTCOME	My husband stormed out and didn't come back for hours. I felt so guilty and still angry. I was on my own then.

TRIGGER	
WARNING SIGN	
ANGER RESPONSE	
OUTCOME	

TRIGGER	
WARNING SIGN	
ANGER RESPONSE	
OUTCOME	

I shall be cool

TRIGGER	
WARNING SIGN	
ANGER RESPONSE	
OUTCOME	

TRIGGER	
WARNING SIGN	
ANGER RESPONSE	
OUTCOME	

TRIGGER	
WARNING SIGN	
ANGER RESPONSE	
OUTCOME	

Destructive anger is like an acid that can do more harm to the vessel in which it is stored than to anything in which it is poured.

Chapter Five
The Umbrella of anger

When we learn to explore our anger on a deeper level, we can often come to an awareness that it was not 'anger' we were feeling at all. It was another feeling that perhaps was prohibited as a child, or a feeling we did not feel comfortable admitting to.

This means that although anger is displayed outwardly, other emotions may be hidden beneath the surface. These other feelings such as sadness, fear, guilt, shame etc might cause a person to feel vulnerable, or they may not have the skills to manage them properly.

By exploring what is underneath the surface of our anger this enables us to gain insight into what is going on for us on an unconscious level. For example if it is anger that we are actually feeling or is it one of the other more complex feelings that we are trying to avoid such as guilt or shame. Some feelings for some of us are somehow unacceptable or more painful to experience.

So, it may be important to explore 'is it really anger the client is feeling, or is it some other feeling?' If we work with the client's anger and it is a feeling hidden under the surface, that they are really feeling, then we are working with a non authentic feeling rather than the real one. Our treatment avenues would then be ineffective.

For example a client who realises that their anger is fuelled by jealousy may benefit from communication skills, whereas a client who realises that their anger is caused by stress will benefit from developing some self care habits.

So as you can see, if we do not explore our anger thoroughly then we can end up working on a phoney feeling and avoid the feeling that we are really feeling.

The Anger Iceberg worksheet on the following page describes the hidden feelings as being below the sea, rather than under the umbrella. Both can be used in multiple ways. It works well as a group discussion piece, or as an activity where clients identify and circle their own hidden emotions. Try the following questions to get started:

Explore the following questions:

- Imagine a friend is facing a situation that is similar to one of your own triggers. What emotions do you think that they might feel other than anger?

- In your family or in the culture you grew up in, what emotions do people freely express? What emotions do they hide?

- Imagine a person who handles difficult emotions, such as sadness, fear or hurt effectively. How do they show these emotions? What do they do to cope with them?

- Anger is sometimes used to mask emotions that make us feel vulnerable, hurt or shame. Can you think of a time you expressed anger in order to conceal another emotion you were feeling?

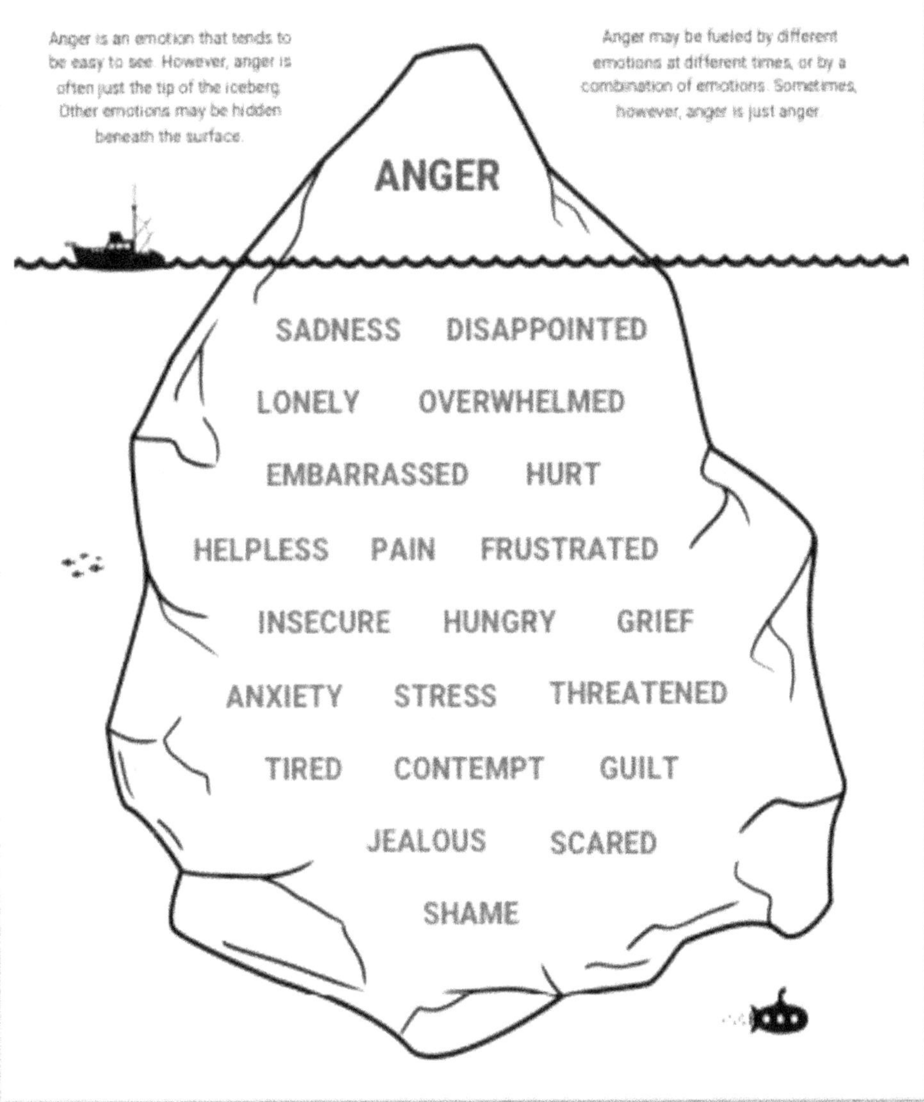
Anger Iceberg

In some families, anger is seen as more acceptable than other emotions. A person might express anger in order to mask emotions that cause them to feel vulnerable, such as hurt or shame.

Anger triggers are people, places, situations, and things that set off anger. Your triggers can provide clues about the emotions behind your anger.

Anger is an emotion that tends to be easy to see. However, anger is often just the tip of the iceberg. Other emotions may be hidden beneath the surface.

Anger may be fueled by different emotions at different times, or by a combination of emotions. Sometimes, however, anger is just anger.

ANGER

SADNESS   DISAPPOINTED

LONELY   OVERWHELMED

EMBARRASSED   HURT

HELPLESS   PAIN   FRUSTRATED

INSECURE   HUNGRY   GRIEF

ANXIETY   STRESS   THREATENED

TIRED   CONTEMPT   GUILT

JEALOUS   SCARED

SHAME

So, your anger may not be an authentic emotion after all in some situations. It might actually be a feeling/emotion that was not encouraged or allowed in your childhood, so you have learned to cover that feeling with another. Equally it may be a learned behaviour to gain attention.

Let me give you an example of a authentic feeling being covered up by a non authentic feeling learned in childhood:

Little Johnny falls over at the age of six and he cries. His Mum tells him to pick himself up, brush himself down and get on, hardly paying him any attention. Each time he is hurt he gets the same old, same old "jump up and shout sugar."

Then he goes to a new school and he feels scared, he becomes upset and Dad says "pull yourself together, and don't be so silly son."

When he plays happily with his friend, he is largely ignored by his parents. But…….. when he kicks off, and screams and shouts throwing his toys everywhere, he suddenly gets a lot of attention.

He gets two messages here – Hurt and Scared is not an acceptable emotion in his little world. However if he gets angry that is okay because 'anger = attention!"

Once that non authentic feeling is in place, it becomes difficult for us to access the authentic feeling that we are really having.

So when Johnny feels hurt or scared when he is told off by his boss at work – he doesn't do scare or hurt emotions very well, they have been suppressed for many years as he was not encouraged to express them as a child. So what does he do…………

Yes, he does anger.

When angry count to ten before you speak, if very angry, count to one hundred.

Chapter Six
Cognitive Techniques for Anger

CBT - Cognitive Behaviour Therapy is currently the evidenced based model for people suffering with depression. However CBT therapists use it with all feelings including 'anger'.

CBT theorists would say that most of the 'bad feelings' we have come from negative thoughts or distortions, and that through identifying the lie behind the thought we can change the way that we feel.

The belief is that thinking, emotions and behaviours intertwine very closely and each can change the others.

So if this is a model that you will find useful, carry on reading, don't discount it though completely, you might find it helpful to try anyway. We already know that our anger can be triggered and that if not dealt with it can escalate into aggression, a loss of temper and/or violence.

The following cycle uses the CBT model to explain how anger grows from an irrational thought and leads to a difficult-to-break cycle of growing frustration.

The Cycle of Anger

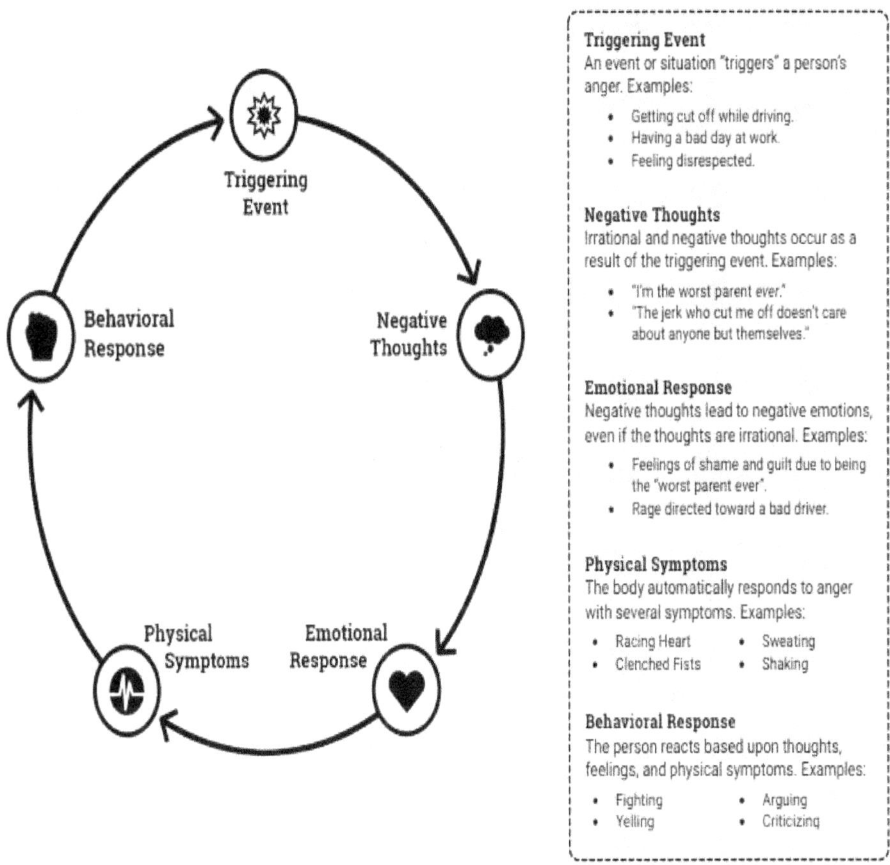

The cycle of anger diagram depicts anger as beginning with a trigger, which leads to negative thoughts, emotions, physical symptoms and a behavioural response.

So, what CBT says is that our thoughts have a huge impact on the way that we feel both emotionally and physically which then influences how we behave. If we are experiencing a lot of negative thoughts then we will feel pretty cranky, and then we may snap at our loved ones.   If we can change our thoughts then evidence shows that we can begin to feel better and behave nicer.

To change our negative thinking, which increases symptoms of stress/depression/anxiety and anger, we need to start by looking at things from different angles. Just like when you want to buy something – say, a new dress or a house – we like to have some alternatives to choose from. This is the same with our thoughts; we need to try generating some alternatives.

To do this we need to develop our 'rational mind.'

RATIONAL MINDS TO THE RESCUE

To prevent the downward spiral in to intense anger, we need to encourage our 'rational' minds to do more work.

Your rational mind likes to look at the evidence. It is 'the detective' if you like. Your rational mind likes to have several alternatives to choose from. Your rational mind likes to test things and run experiments. Your rational mind does not jump to hasty conclusions

Last but not least your rational mind knows that we learn more from trial and error, from our mistakes and not our successes

EXERCISE

I would now like you to use compassion to change your mind about any negative thoughts that have popped up for you. I need you to write these thoughts down. If possible try and use a thought that makes you feel angry.

We can have several thoughts and feelings about ourselves, some of which can be quite critical and harsh. These thoughts and feelings can lead to more distress.

When you have written down your negative thoughts I would like you to look at each negative thought and ask yourself the following questions:

1. What are the advantages of this self criticism?
2. What are the disadvantages of this self criticism?
3. Where will this self criticism eventually lead you?
4. What sort of person will it turn you into?
5. What is your greatest fear in giving up this self criticism?
6. What might others gain from you staying self critical?

Now let us look at the origins of this self attacking style and why people continue and submit or agree to it and why (e.g. habit, or fear based)?

1. When did you start to become self critical?
2. What was happening in your life?

3. Whose voice started the process?

4. What would have been your greatest fear in standing up to that critical other or voice in your head?

5. What would it take now to stop agreeing with it?

6. What are the credentials of this critic (external or internal?)

7. Does your inner critic have your best loving interests at heart?

Once you have done this explore ways in which you can disentangle yourself from your inner critic.

Remember your thoughts can trigger negative emotions, physical symptoms which then can affect the way that we behave.

If the video goes wrong, we troubleshoot. If our business is failing, we troubleshoot. How many of us actually troubleshoot our own lives. It's because of this that the same horrible things happen to us time and time again. We don't stop to ask why???

Let's troubleshoot now. Imagine you had the following belief:

"The world is a crap place to live in" **or** *"I am a worthless person"*

This belief could affect the way that you feel, the way that you behave and increase your feelings of anger. Of course it is a LIE!

The world is not always a crap place to live in and you are far from worthless! Let's look at what this cycle of thought may create using what CBT therapists call 'the hot cross bun or the CBT cycle:

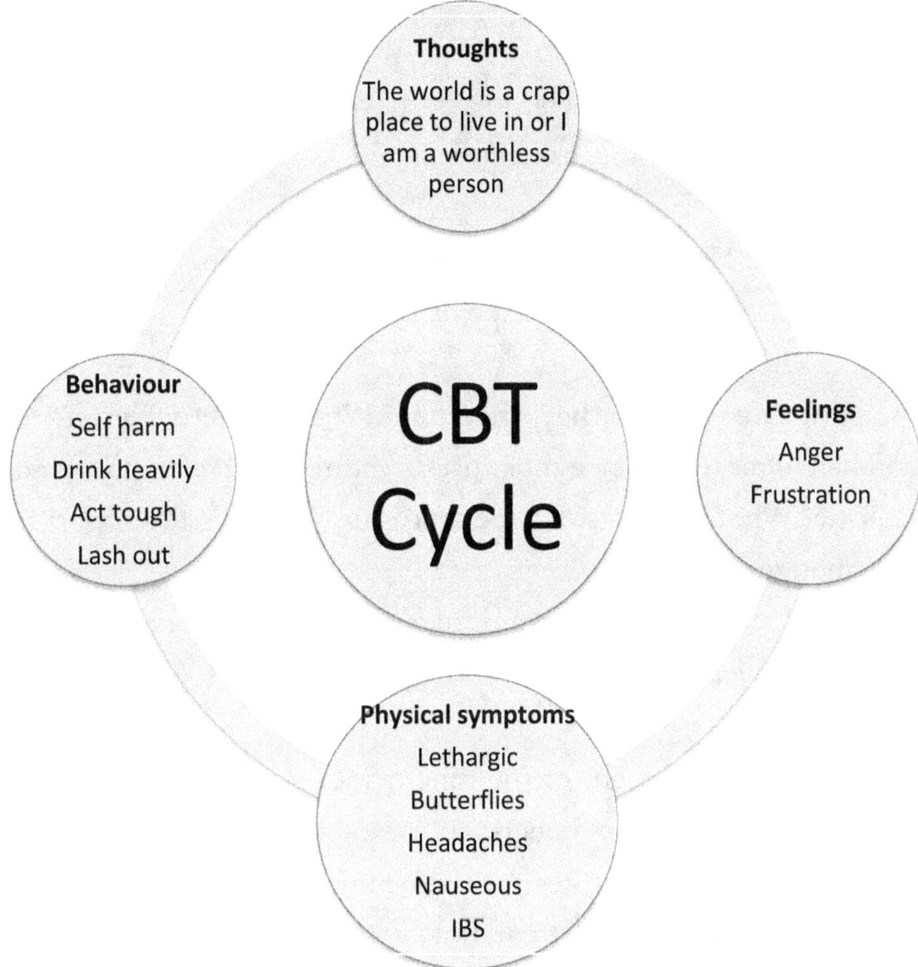

Your thoughts will trigger the negative feelings, which will leave you feeling physically unwell, and subsequently impact on your behaviour. This in turn may set you up for further pain. This will subsequently reinforce the negative thought process.

In other words 'wonky thinking' leads to 'wonky feelings' and these produce unhealthy behaviours.

EXERCISE

What beliefs do you have? List some of your own negative thoughts. Now ask yourself:

1.   How helpful are these thoughts to you?
2.   How do they help with your anger?

Now check out if they are true? Where's the evidence? Ask yourself what would be a more useful thought or belief that is more realistic? What evidence or experiences do you have to support this new thought or belief?

Draw yourself a diagram like the example and see what feelings, physical symptoms and behaviours that your thoughts trigger.

Ninety nine percent of the time evidence will show that your negative thoughts or beliefs to be a 'lie!' And yet these thoughts/beliefs, these 'lies' are affecting the way that you feel, emotionally and physically and how you behave,

They are not supportive of your anger management plan.

Once you have reality tested your negative thoughts and sought out the truth, look what happens then. Look at the difference this new; more realistic thought would have on feelings, physical symptoms and behaviour:

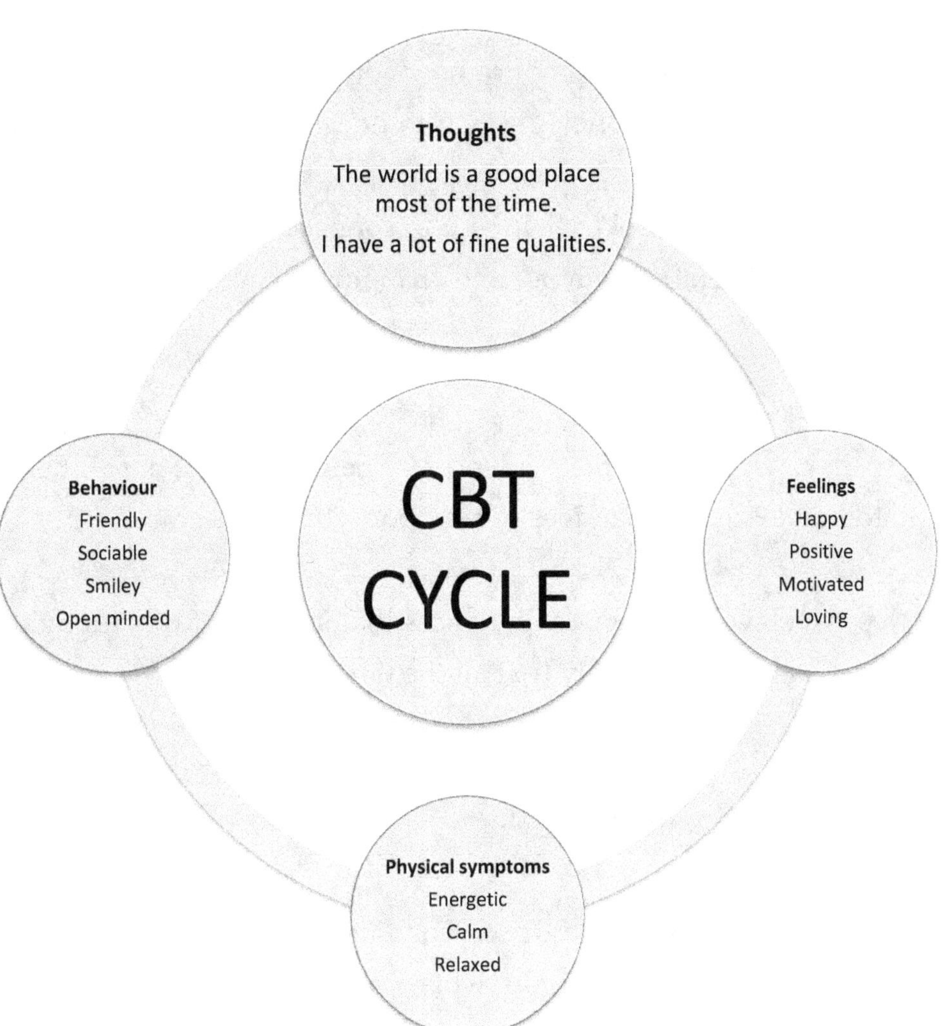

A new belief, a more realistic belief will change your feelings and behaviour. A new belief, a more realistic belief will change your feelings and behaviour.

"Your life is what your thoughts make it" - **Marcus Aurelius**

Think about all your negative thoughts and practice changing them using this model, and notice how your feelings and behaviour change too. Apart from helping you to develop healthier beliefs, it can be fun.

Here is another tool to help you to connect with your thoughts and practice checking them out and changing them:

EXERCISE

Where's the evidence?   These are questions to help you to find evidence that does not support your thought:

- Have I had any experiences that show that this thought is not completely true all the time?

- If my best friend or someone I loved had this thought, what would I tell them?

- If my best friend or someone who loves me knew I was thinking this thought, what would they say to me?

- What evidence would they point out to me that would suggest that my thoughts were not 100% true?

- When I am not feeling this way, do I think about this type of situation any differently? How?

- When I have felt this way in the past, what did I think about that helped me to feel better?

- Five years from now, if I look back at this situation, will I look at it any differently?

- Are there any strengths or positives in me or the situation that I am ignoring?

- Am I jumping to any conclusions that are not completely justified by the evidence?

- Am I blaming myself for something over which I do not have complete control?

I am now going to show you some exit points to get off this cycle of anger, which can be used for any negative thoughts even those that cause you to feel depressed or anxious too.

All cycles can be stepped off, everyone has the ability to change the way that they think feel and behave.

Here is the cycle again, this time with exit points. Followed by some tools to use at each exit point:

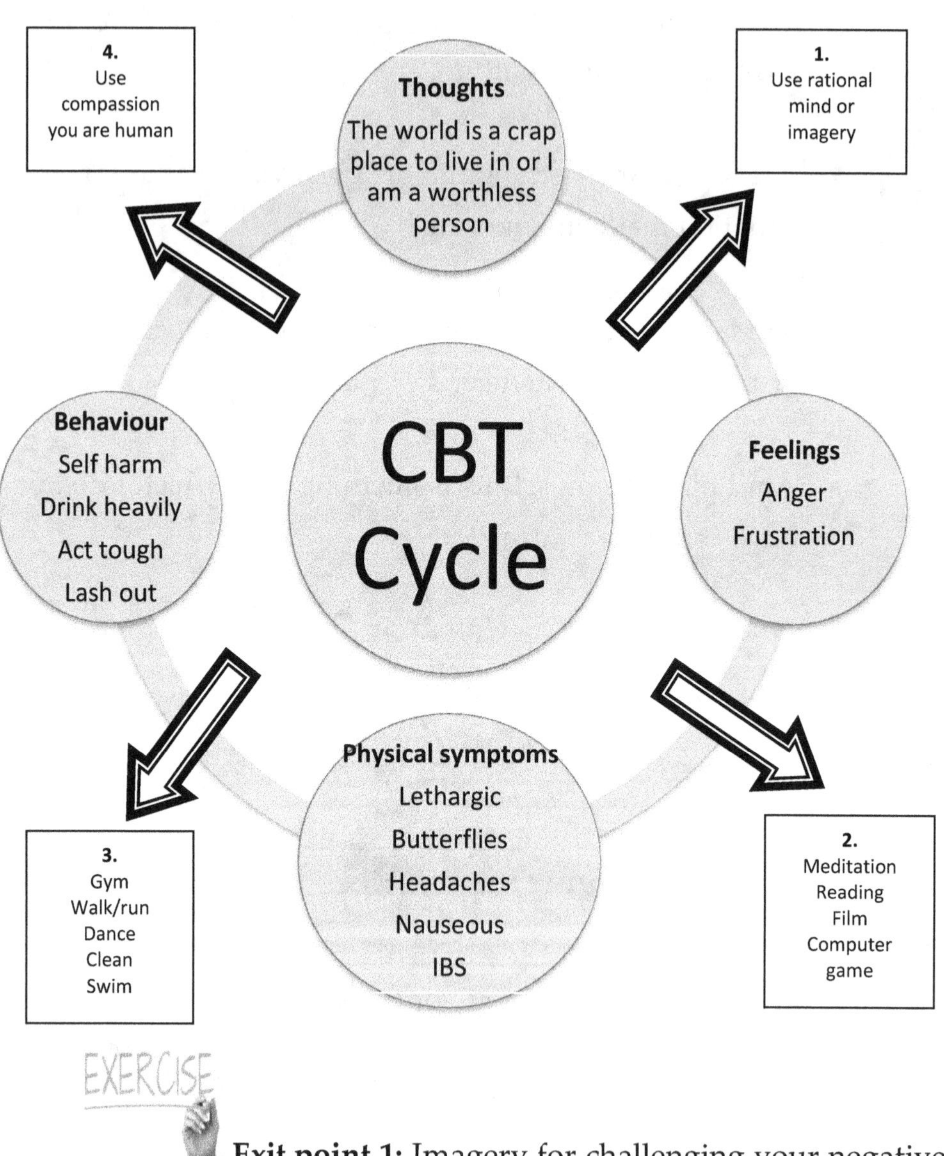

Exit point 1: Imagery for challenging your negative thoughts.

Firstly I need you to think about someone famous, this may be an actress, politician, sports personality or comedian that you really do not like, that you think talks a lot of rubbish (bear in mind this will be your perception).

If this person entered the room you would walk out, because nothing s/he said would be interesting, honest or make any sense. Let's use mine and bear in mind, (I cannot use real celebrities names in this book for obvious reasons, so I will use a pseudo name)

JANET POTTER

Now I'd like you to think of someone, who you admire and feel, talks a lot of sense, someone whom you could sit and listen to for hours. I will use:

CHERYL COLLINS

Now choose your own.

The first person (*in my example Janet Potter*) is your negative thoughts, your critical self, you internal bully.

The second person (*in my example Cheryl Collins*) is your positive thoughts, your nurturing self, the self that will challenge bullies, and challenge the things that are not the truth.

Now think about one of your negative thoughts, again I will use one of my own:

Linda, you are not a very nice person, you shouted at your children today

Now say to yourself "NO this is (your bullying person) Janet Potter speaking, before I believe this I will ask what (your nurturing person) Cheryl Collins thinks, Cheryl says:

Linda, everyone shouts at their kids sometimes and it is natural that you feel guilty, but most of the time you are brilliant with your kids

Which thought should I listen to? Which thought is the truth? If I listened to 'Janet Potter' I would feel low, lethargic, and angry, disappointed all day and may even lash out in anger.

If I listen to Cheryl then I will feel good, energized, motivated and calm.

It is quite clear which of these statements are the truth and yet most of us choose to listen to the lie, most of us will not challenge the lie.

Before listening and accepting what your first person has said ask yourself what the second person would say then make a choice which one is telling the truth. We don't have to accept what our negative thinking (our internal bully) says, so stop listening to your internal bully!

In this exercise you could use animals instead of people, cartoon characters or any imagery that works for you.

A good idea is to print off several copies of your 'nurturing' person/animal and stick them on the fridge, your wardrobe door, your bathroom mirror, your desk, and in your car or even as your screen savers on your mobile phone and computer, as a reminder to 'check out' that negative thought with your nurturing person before believing it.

The important thing is to believe in what your nurturing self says, this is the 'person' most likely to be telling the TRUTH!

If you are thinking more positive about yourself, then your self esteem will be good, and you will not feel so angry.

These tools and techniques I am sharing with you, need you to try them for them to work. If you really want to manage your anger more productively, you need to do the work.

Here is another imagery you could use. You may have heard about the 'devil' that you have on one shoulder and the 'angel' that you have on the other:

Challenge the thoughts on the left by thinking about what your fairy godmother would say and write these down on the right.

Negative thoughts	Positive thoughts

By challenging your thoughts using what works best for you, will change the way that you are feeling both physically and emotionally. This in turn will change the way that you behave.

In terms of anger, if you change your thought to a more positive, a more truthful one then your feelings will improve and you will be more motivated to do things. **Try it and see.**

EXERCISE

Exit point 2: If you have missed challenging your negative thoughts and the feeling kicks in, then you may need to use tools and techniques to calm down those feelings such as:

- ✓ Meditation
- ✓ Relaxation Techiniques
- ✓ Mindfullness
- ✓ Reading
- ✓ Watching a film
- ✓ Having a massage
- ✓ Bubble bath and early night
- ✓ Rub your tummy and say the words "I will take care of you, I will protect you."
- ✓ Play some music
- ✓ Play a computor game or board game

All these tools will calm down your anger. Also you could put a comedy on, remember you can only feel one feeling at one time, if you are laughing at a comedy, then you are not going to be feeling angry are you.

EXERCISE

Exit point 3:   If you have missed the exit points at thoughts, and feelings and the physical symptoms kick in, then of course the tools at exit points 1 and 2 may not be powerful enough. Once the physical symptoms kick in, you will need something physical to calm these down, such as:

- ✓ Going to the gym
- ✓ Swimming
- ✓ Walking/running
- ✓ Jogging on the spot
- ✓ Dancing
- ✓ Cleaning
- ✓ Running up and down the stairs
- ✓ Yoga
- ✓ Kickboxing
- ✓ Press ups
- ✓ Trampolining

All these will help to calm down your physical symptoms.

EXERCISE

Exit point 4: Its not unusual especially when beginning to so this type of work that you forget to use these tools and techiniques and end up doing the full cycle. That is okay, it takes time. There is only one tool at this stage and that is to be compassionate towards yourself. You are human and this is sometimes the way we mere mortals function. Perhaps you could write yourself a compassionate letter and forgive yourself.

Your anger may still at some point need to be dealt with, processed and if necessary addressed. These tools are to help you to calm down first.

It is more difficult to process and express in a constructive way if you are in the midst of overwhelming anger or rage. So the important thing when learning how to manage anger effectively is to cool down first.

I would like you to put this book down and process your thoughts, using any or all of the tools described in this chapter try and check out the honesty behind your negative thoughts, use the tools for any negative feeling as practice for when you feel angry.

Enjoy this new way of being.

When you let anger get the best of you, it brings out the worst of you.

Chapter Seven
Transactional analysis and anger

This is one of the most important chapters in the book. It is my view that with this chapter alone if you practice the technique you will see massive changes in being able to manage your anger in a more constructive way. Even if you are dealing with angry people by changing your communication style, this will facilitate the change in self and others.

Humans have a very special weapon, a very unique talent and that is the ability to 'hook into' other people's emotions, more often than not (unless they are cruel) they do this on an unconscious level. This is because they are not aware of our 'crumple buttons'. These are emotions and behaviours that can trigger something painful from our own past.

Other people can 'hook' into our inner child and leave us feeling very angry. This is the part of us that is most vulnerable. They are not always aware that they are doing this as they are not always aware of other peoples own internal process.

Learning about this model, helped me considerably in being able to own my 'own stuff' and manage my own anger in a healthier way.   It prevented other people from hooking into my emotions, and helped me to stay calm and in control.   This secret technique that can help you too is the 'ego-state model' which comes from a model of therapy called 'Transactional Analysis 'founded by Eric Berne.

Transactional Analysis is an analysis of our own transactions, (non verbal and verbal communications). It helps us to explore why sometimes our way of transacting can cause more problems than good. It can also be used to change your feelings, behaviour and ways of relating too, and is a great tool for improving our relationships with others.

The theory of transactional analysis is that we all have three parts which Eric Berne calls 'ego states'. We have a parent ego-state, an adult ego state and a child ego state.

We slip in and out of these states throughout the day. Right now I am in my Nurturing Parent ego state because I am teaching you. If I was in my child ego state then I might be sulking because my needs are not being met. I may even start to get angry. I may even slip into my adult ego state and become very rational.

I have a choice I can stay in my child ego state and lash out at my loved ones or even throw a plate at one of them OR I can shift into my adult ego state and deal with the problem in a healthy and constructive way. If the person I am in confrontation with is in his or her child ego state too, then s/he has a choice too either stay in child ego state or shift into adult like me and resolve the issue in a mature way.

This is the diagram of the ego state model.

Ego state model

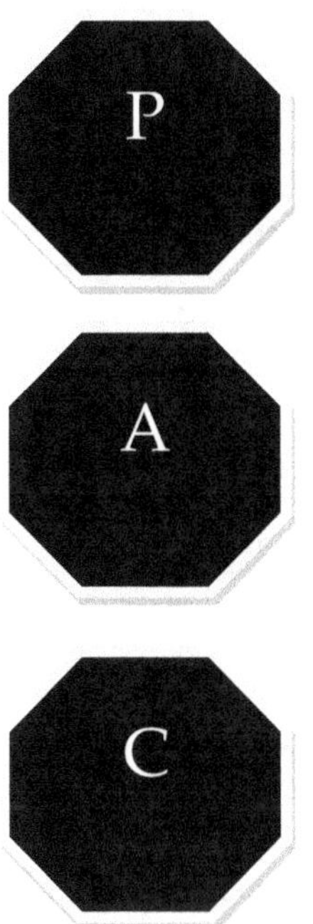

Eric Berne believes that we move in and out of these states during our daily lives and during various situations, feelings and thoughts. (Different transactions)

Up until now this has probably been 'out of your awareness', however learning about ego-states enables us to bring this into 'our awareness', which can help us to form healthier relationships and think and behave in healthy ways.

We have possibly all experienced those times where we have been that frustrated and angry with other people's behaviour that we have 'lost it' with them, shouted and screamed at them, and then felt awful afterwards. It can leave us feeling that we have lost control. So let's learn how to manage this differently:

During any transaction when we are in our parent ego state, we feel, think and behave as our own parents or caretakers did. This is where our learned behaviour comes from in terms of how they managed their anger. This is where our transactions could be critical or nurturing, both externally and internally.

When we are in our child ego state we feel, think and behave as we did as children, although sometimes in a more adult way. This is the state we may be in when our transactions are sulky and argumentative.

However, when we are in our adult ego state we behave in a more constructive fashion.

This is when we do our reality testing and logical thinking. In adult we deal with situations in the 'here and now' without letting past or future issues cloud our judgement.

EXERCISE

It will be helpful if you spend some time analysing which ego state that you are in at different times of the day and in different situations. This brings you to more awareness of ego states.

You can have some fun in analysing yourself and others, you may get it wrong but that is okay. It takes practice. Watch the soaps it is great fun analysing the characters in them too.

One of the common mistakes when people are doing this work is to confuse their parent ego state with their adult.

The more that you practice and incorporate this into your daily lives, the better and easier at it you will become. Remember all ego states are healthy when in the right one at the right time.

To help you along the way, here are a few tips:

<u>CHILD EGO STATE</u> is when we are hurting, sulking, fighting, arguing, or hurting other people. It is when we are throwing tantrums, slamming doors, acting the goat, playing psychological games, or being the victim.

It is when we are unassertive, have a low self-esteem, embarrassed, feeling good, silly, and bad, bullying, teasing and joking. It is all the things we did, as children so be it sometimes in an adult way.

This is the ego-state others may try to hook in to. It is where you carry all your own emotions, and the minute that others hook into this during a confrontation you have lost the battle! Because you will more than likely throw a tantrum just as you did as a kid or lose control, unless of course, you are able to remain in your adult ego state.

The child ego state is also the ego state where you store your anger from your past, so that when other people trigger a past incident that caused you to feel angry, you are likely to transfer the anger with the person in the past on to the person in the current situation and dump the whole lot on him or her.

<u>PARENT EGO STATE</u> is when we are scolding, criticising, praising, dictating, persecuting, teaching, nursing or nurturing self and others. It is all the things we can remember our own caretakers doing. Remember that we will have a critical parent and a positive parent. This can be internally or externally. Be mindful that our dictating parent ego state can come out too when in conflict, so that's not helpful either. We do have to be in our parent ego state when nurturing, setting clear boundaries and consequences.

<u>ADULT EGO STATE</u> is when we are calm, rational, thinking logically and reality testing. It is when we deal with our own and others emotions constructively. It is when we are comfortable, okay, non judgmental accepting and honest. It is the ego state we often try to stay in, in our work environment.

The adult ego state is the ego state that helps us to manage our negative feelings of frustration and anger and prevents us from acting out our negative emotions. The adult ego state is non-threatening.

When dealing with a confrontation or our own feelings of anger, if we can manage to shift our self into the right ego state then we will be able to handle things such as our own feelings, fears and behaviour in a much more constructive way.

I must emphasise stay out of your child ego state, when feeling angry or facing someone else's anger.

When communicating in anger the black arrows demonstrate the unhealthy ego states to be communicating in.

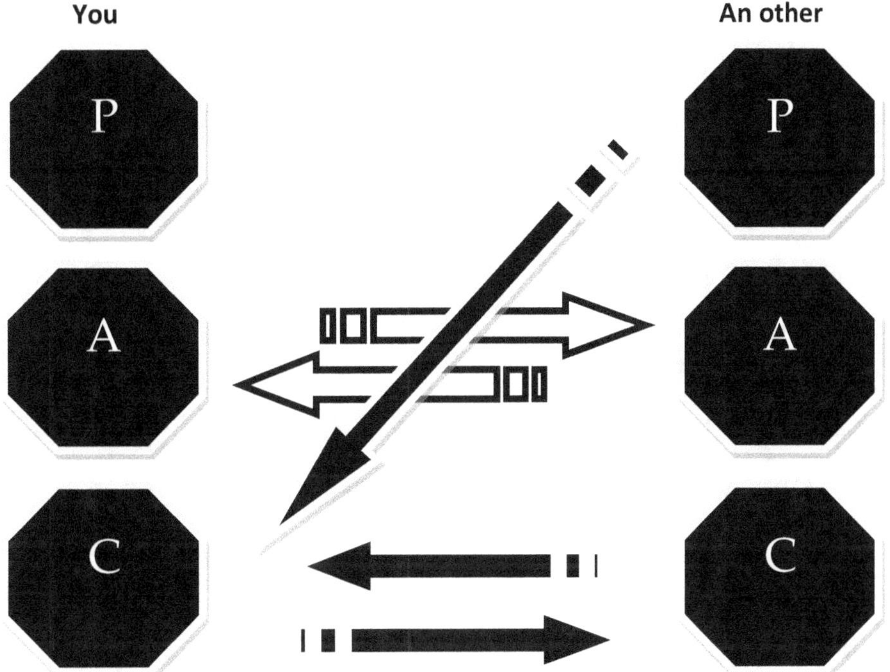

BLACK ARROW - This is the position where someone may be hooking into your child from his or her parent ego state or where you are both communicating from child ego state. Or if addressing someone from a critical parent then that can trigger other peoples anger too. The healthy position is to both communicate from a adult to adult in situations that are confrontational. An example of that is:

You: "It's going to snow"

Another: "Don't be so blooming stupid, it's not going to snow. You are just making excuses" **(Parent ego state)**

You: "Don't call me stupid, you ugly person. I have a right to my own opinion." **(Child ego state)**

Another: "That's it I'm not going now, you can go on your own, I'm not going anywhere again" **(Child ego state)**

So, the conversation started off Parent to Child ego state and then ended up in Child to Child' – something small turned into something big with both parties communicating in an unhealthy way.

An argument is bound to follow this kind of interaction, which will deplete you both of psychological energy.

WHITE ARROWS - Look how this might have been very different if both parties had stayed in an Adult to Adult transaction:

You: "It's going to snow"

Another: "Do you think so, what do you want to do?"

You: "Shall we leave it until the weather picks up?"

Another: "Yes, shall we watch a film instead?"

This way of communicating helps you to hang on to your energy, and prevents the situation from blowing into a full scale row, that hovers over the relationship all day, or sometimes days.

All ego states are healthy as long as we are in them at the right time in the right situation. We can learn how to manage our ego states so that we are. It takes time and practice but is great fun doing and leads us to a calmer life.

Don't lose the spirit of your child ego state, this is the state that encourages your spontaneity and has fun, just pack him/her away when in the midst of an argument or confrontation.

When we are in Parent ego state we act, feel and think as our parents/caretaker did both internally and externally. If we had an extremely critical parent then it is very likely that we become self critical when we are adults and critical of others. Critical people are more prone to anger.

Those that have a strong nurturing parent learned from childhood then they are less likely to be angry people.

Then we have our child ego state which is when we act, feel and think as we did as children. If we sulked as a child to get our needs met then we will most likely sulk as grownups too, when our needs are not being met. This is the ego state that 'tries to be perfect' or 'people pleases,' this can leave us angry because it leaves us feeling worn out and unable to manage our anger effectively. We cannot be perfect or please everyone all of the time.   People who accept their imperfections and are more assertive are less likely to be angry individuals..

The Adult ego state is 'the rational mind,' this is where we do our logical thinking and reality testing. This is the part of us that is stable and makes healthy decisions and choices. This part of us is far able to manage anger in a constructive way.

So in a nutshell, the inner child part of us will see a bar of chocolate and steal it. The inner critical Parent will stop us and say "Don't do that you idiot!", the inner nurturing Parent will say "Let's explore what might happen if you stole that chocolate honey." The Adult would reality test this with you and look at all the possible consequences of stealing the chocolate.

Don't forget we move in and out of these states throughout the day and throughout our lives. Often when we are in conflict and it turns out bad we have responded /reacted from our Child ego state.

All our emotions are in our Child ego state and our unconscious processes and memories, most importantly when we are angry we spend a lot of our time there.

When we are angry we listen to our inner critic (Critical Parent) all the time and ignore the Nurturing part of us or the rational part of us (Adult).   Being in child is great when we are having fun with our significant others but not when we are angry it renders us stuck there.

EXERCISE

Spend some time looking back over recent events and think about what ego- state you might have been in. Over the next day or so try using your inner Parent to nurture yourself and your Adult ego state to rationalise all of those irrational thoughts.

(If you like this model there is a lot of books on the market that teaches you more. One of my favourites is 'Counselling for Toads" by Robert De Board. It is easy reading and is about Toad from Wind in the Willows who is depressed and angry. He goes to see a TA therapist and is helped with his anger and depression).

Explain your anger
instead of acting out on it
and you will find
Solutions and
Connections,
instead of arguments.

Chapter Eight
Letting go of historical anger

Have you ever wondered why what makes you angry doesn't always make other people angry and vice versa.   This is because we all have different psychopathologies. We all have our own internal processes. We have all had different experiences and even those that have the same or similar experiences to ourselves will have different interpretations of that experience.   So we are all unique but different.

Memories of traumatic or enraging events can trigger angry feelings, particularly if a recent incident has triggered historical anger. For example a client has been bullied at school; he then experiences real or imagined bullying at work. This may resurrect old feelings from the past which s/he may act out in the present.

Some of the anger that s/he is feeling may be unresolved anger from the past. If you can make those links between past and present then this may reduce the intensity of feeling.

Sometimes I may facilitate the client in writing a letter to the 'past' bullies or people they are angry with, to enable them to let go of those feelings from the past and focus on the current 'here and now' anger. The letter would be destroyed afterwards. I explain that our bodies do not know how we release that anger; just that it has been released. A little like stress, the body is unable to distinguish between a physical release to the 'bullies' from the past and a psychological release to the bullies from the past.

Ask them to imagine the unresolved anger as a jug of water inside of them, which is overflowing. Writing the letter helps them to empty that jug. If it is full of unresolved anger then one is more likely to have repetitive outbursts.

The instinctive or natural way to express anger is to respond aggressively. We tend to feel the emotion and then act on it. You don't have to do that. Sit with it for awhile until it calms right down (or distract yourself if you are unable to sit with it).

There are a variety of reasons a person may become angry, which I have discussed throughout this book, one thing I haven't covered yet is our expectations of self or others. This can be a big trigger for anger towards self or others. We may have had high expectations placed on us as children. We may still have those now of ourselves. If we set too high expectations on self or others, then we can feel angry when those expectations are not met towards our self or others.

Hooking into our pasts

It is very easy for others to 'hook into our past pain" mostly unconsciously (as they don't know what our crumple buttons are) or occasionally some people will do this consciously (because they want to kick our crumple buttons).

What makes one person crumple, will not affect another, that is because we all have different crumple buttons linked to what we have experienced in our past.

For example, if we have experienced real or imagined rejection in our past then this can be extremely painful when we experience real or imagined rejection in our current relationships. Of course, when we are in pain, we act out on that pain, often in anger.

These are things that will trigger our anger and often surprise people at the intensity of our anger because in a sense they have splattered open an old wound.

Imagine a child that has been lied to, this lie caused them great pain. It is inevitable that lies are going to be a crumple button for them in all their relationships as an adult. This would be their crumple button. Therefore to be lied to would be likely to cause them intense anger.

Ask yourself have you ever been shocked in a relationship when someone has exploded at something you have said or done? This is maybe because unintentionally you have 'hooked a crumple button most probably from their past.' We are all unique with our own unique pasts, and equally we all make our own interpretations of those experiences.

Think about your own 'crumple buttons'

1. What really makes you angry?
2. What really hurts you?
3. What causes you intense anger or pain?
4. Can you recall the last time you exploded?
5. What happened?
6. What did the person say or do?
7. Can you recall a time in your past when this happened to you?

This can happen to all of us at times, it is often what we struggle to understand in others, when we see them 'flip' over what we deem to be the smallest of things. It maybe that for them it has 'hooked into something from their past.' (Of course it maybe the straw that broke the camel's back too, if they are stressed).

The idea once you are aware, is to separate the past from the present. Roll with the feeling before acting on it. Ask yourself "what has this hooked into?"

For example if it is rejection or being lied to and it does link to the past, deal with the rejection or lie in the 'here and now.' This is not xyz, this is this person rejecting me or lying to me. Of course, this may not be acceptable behaviour and you may want to address it, but separating it from your past anger and pain will help you to deal with it productively.

To be able to resolve issues from the past in therapy may leave you less likely to experience intense anger in your current situations.

Anger and our belief system

I would now like to talk about how a person's belief system can cause strong feelings of Anger, which is based on the work of Albert Ellis the founder of rational emotive behaviour therapy.

First of all let's do the following exercise:

Exploring beliefs:

1. What are your beliefs?
2. Which ones do you hold on tightly too?
3. Which beliefs do you have that do not help you?
4. Which beliefs do you hold that cause you more harm than good?

A belief is something that you think is the truth. It can be thought of as a list of "should" and "should nots." For example "I should be able to do this job, without it overwhelming me."

Many of these beliefs are formed when you are a child. They can come from covert or overt messages that you hear from your parents. They can be instilled by a parent, teacher or other significant person in your life. Sometimes these teachings are a valuable asset but sometimes they can cause you problems later in your life.

"If at first you don't succeed, try and try again" is one for example. Sometimes it might be just as helpful to walk away and try something different. However this instilled belief can wear you out and cause you to feel like a failure when you don't succeed, subsequently making you feel angry.

Irrational beliefs are more likely to cause you greater problems and anger than rational ones. Knowing that you do not have to keep pushing yourself to succeed in something can leave you feeling calmer.

The next time you become upset and/or angry, take a look at what belief you have that is making you feel this way. Then ask yourself "Is my belief rational?" More often than not the belief is not practical or rational. Once you are able to recognise the problem with your belief, then you can make an adjustment as needed.

If you recognise that the belief is not rational and that it heightens your anger with yourself and others then you will be able to change it or adjust it to make you feel calmer.

"If at first I don't succeed, it is okay sometimes to stop trying and try something else."

Another adjustment may be to add some level of understanding to that belief. So if you believe that you should always be treated fairly then when someone treats you unfairly this can leave you feeling angry. You could adjust that belief to 'most people will treat me fairly in life, but there will always be some that will not and will take advantage of me – that's life!"

However, there may be times when you might process your belief and recognise that it is rational. That is okay. Testing your beliefs tell you when your anger is justifiable. Anger is normal don't forget. It is okay to then express your anger in a healthy way. You will learn how to do this later on in this book. Not all beliefs are irrational, so you may need to address them.

It is important to remember that when anger is justified to learn to use the energy in a positive way, instead of being violent, verbally abusive, or doing something else that will result in harming yourself and/or harming others.

Anger runs in families

Anger often runs in families. Think back to how your parents, grandparents and other extended family expressed their anger. Were they 'angry people?'

Some people believe that 'anger' and the way we express it is genetic. Ask yourself these questions:

- Are we born angry?
- Do we come out of our mother's womb saying, "all men/women are bad?"
- Do we lash out in anger because we believe we are treated unfairly?

No, we cry when we are hungry or in pain, not because we are angry. Although some people may see this is 'anger'. Most experts agree that anger and the way that we express it is a learned behaviour. A family teaches a child how to express feelings such as being sad, scared and angry. If our parents do not handle anger appropriately then as a child we are likely to handle it in the same way. Without any teaching of how to express our anger in a constructive way, then we may grow into adults that continue to express anger negatively.

Not all parents are perfect; maybe they have not been taught how to express anger in a healthy way. Don't forget they have been taught by their parents too. These behaviours are passed down from generation to generation, almost like an heirloom. We can change this; we can throw that unwanted heirloom away and deal with our anger differently. Everyone has the ability to change.

You are a role model for your children, the way that you express anger they will learn to do the same. You can decide to break the cycle of anger that is being passed along through generations. Think about how great it would be to help the next generation of your family to give them a calmer and peaceful life.

When your family members become angry, take the time to talk to them about their feelings. Accept their feelings as normal. Help them to express those feelings by staying calm and listening. Remember from earlier in the book that anger may not be their real feelings.   It is important to create an environment where all members can talk freely about their emotions without being judged.

Start by taking steps to reduce your own anger.   Anger is energy for something productive or destructive. It is your choice if you use it productively or destructively an as like all choices we have to then take responsibility for the choices we make.

Ask yourself will it matter tomorrow?   Next week?   Next Month?   Are you allowing others to 'make' you angry?   No one can 'make' you feel anything. Those feelings are yours. If you allow someone to 'make' you feel angry, you are allowing them to control you.   Do you really want others to control you, pull your strings?

The only one responsible for your anger is you. Use the energy wisely

Do not look upon anger as something foreign that you have to fight,

Look upon it as something you have to deal with, with care, with love and with tenderness and most importantly with non violence.

Chapter Nine
Stress and anger

If another can easily anger you, it is because you are off balance with yourself. You may be feeling stressed or burnt out. Stress is more prevalent today than twenty years ago; it is no coincidence then that there is also more anger, such as road rage, workplace violence, fights outside pubs etc.

If you are prone to anger, then stress is more likely to increase your angry behaviours.

Stress (like anger) is healthy when you have good stress management techniques. It is what gets us out of bed in the morning and gets us through our working day. This type of stress does not usually cause us anger or irritability. Some people actually thrive on this type of stress.

However, distress is a type of stress that can cause people to be irritable and/or angry. This happens when our stress levels get too high. This is when there is a combination of stressors and where things are piling up. Eventually this builds and builds until the person cannot handle all the stressors, they then have an angry outburst.

Stress is primarily a physical response. When stressed, the body thinks it is under attack and switches to 'fight or flight' mode, releasing a complex of hormones and chemicals such as adrenaline, cortisol and norepinephrine to prepare the body for physical action.

Through the release of these hormones the caveman gained a rush of energy, which prepared him to either fight the tiger or run away. The heart pounds, breathing becomes faster and there is a boost of energy. It enables us to focus our attention so we can quickly respond to the situation.

In the modern world, the fight or flight mode can still help us to survive dangerous situations, such as reacting swiftly to a person running in front of our car by slamming on the brakes.

It is when our body goes into a state of stress in inappropriate situations whereby we are not in danger that it becomes problematic. The blood flow is going to the most important muscles needed to fight or run; brain function is minimised leading to an inability to think straight. This leaves us unable to function in both our work and home lives.

When your body goes into a state of stress, we may feel agitated and aggressive towards others; this can be due to our bodies' natural reaction being 'fight.' We instantly will need to release the adrenalin to feel better. This can be a helpful reaction to ward off predators, but in unnecessary situations, we can release that adrenalin on other people unnecessarily. It can negatively affect relationships and ruin reputations.

As with anger we need to explore if stress is the authentic feeling as it could be another feeling that you do not feel comfortable in expressing such as overwhelmed, disrespected, helpless, scared etc.

We need to look at why we are having this reaction. What is happening in our life? Are we taking on too much? Are we scared to say 'No?' Why are we scared to say 'No?' What do we fear if we say 'No?' Are we trying to be perfect? Why? What will happen if we just be good enough? What do we fear by just being 'good enough?'

All these things can lead to a stress reaction and subsequently in some instances an angry outburst.

Once you have identified the feelings and thoughts associated with your stress, take a look at your environment. Do you live in a chaotic home environment or perhaps have a work environment that is adding to your stress? When you identify your environmental stressors, take some time to identify ways to limit those stressors in addition to changing the ways you are thinking.

Once this insight is gained, then steps can be taken to relax, take better care of ourselves and enable us to feel much better.

Firstly let's look at if you are doing too much.

On the following page is a tool to explore what is causing your stress and how to do more self nurturing and relaxation type strategies to help you to manage your stress in a healthier way.

As you will see there is a picture of a clown. Around his feet you will see balloons. These are **'lead weight'** balloons. Write in these balloons all the things that you do or have in your life that you would deem stressful.

For example you may put work, children, ill parent or debts, bad neighbours.

Once you have done this fill in the balloons around the clown's neck. These are **'helium balloons'.** Write in these balloons all the things you do or have for relaxation. This may be the gym, reading, dance classes or bubble baths, an exercise bike.

You will probably notice that you will struggle to fill in all of these balloons compared to the 'lead weight' balloons.

"For every 'lead weight' balloon that you have around your feet, you need <u>two</u> 'helium balloons' to hold them up"

It is doubtful that you have this equivalent so you can now see why you are feeling so stressed and subsequently angry. This demonstrates that you need to find more relaxation techniques to keep your stress and anger levels more healthily balanced.

Remember the more stressed you are, the more you are likely to become angry and the less likely that you will be able to manage this anger productively.

I shall be cool

Stress balloons

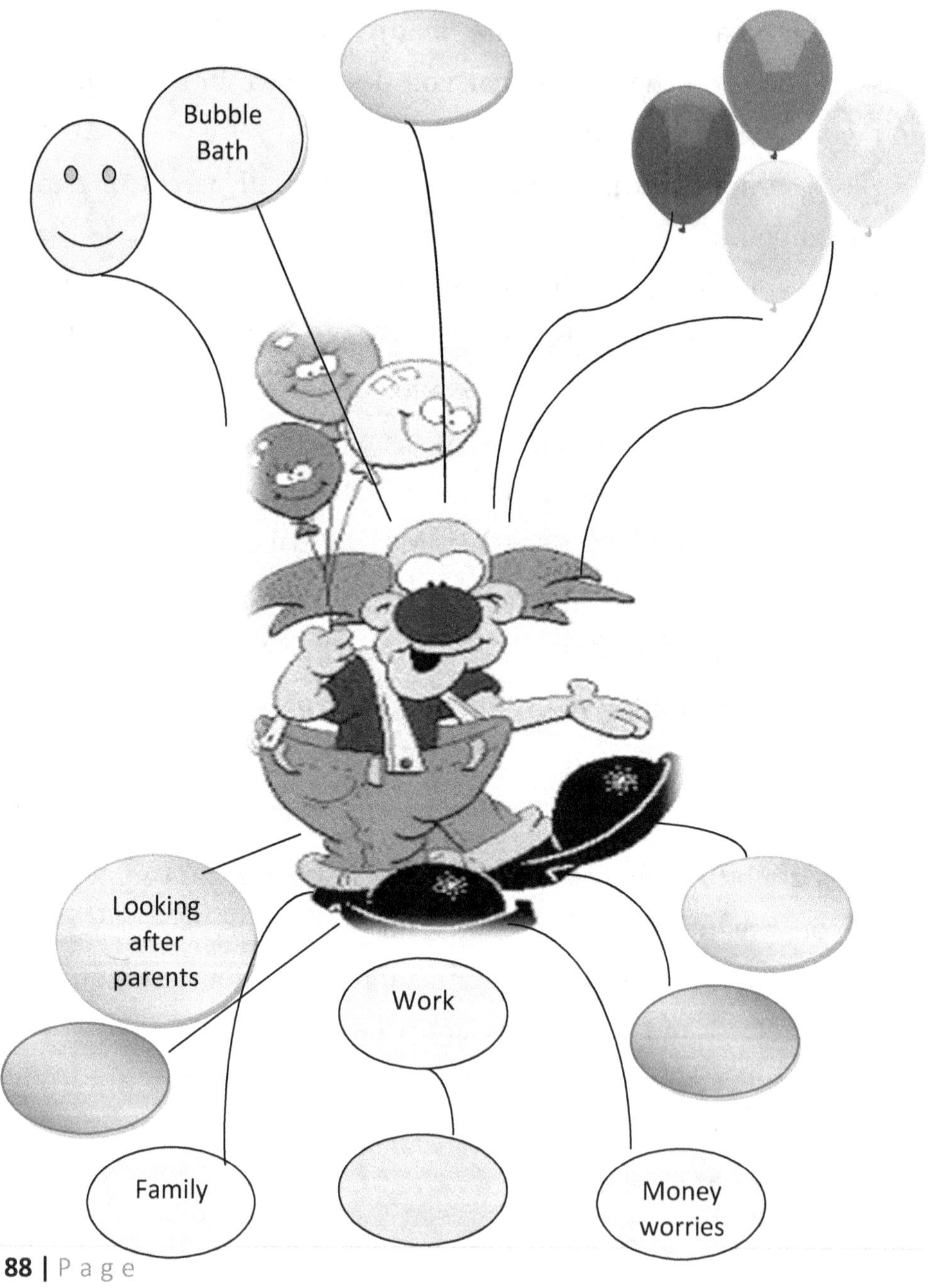

Stress Management techniques:

Below are some ways in which you may manage your stress. Find some of your own too.

- Change your thinking
- Change your behaviour
- Change your lifestyle
- Be assertive
- Get organised/Time management
- Get plenty fresh air
- Use humour
- Appreciate yourself and others more easily
- Be imperfect
- Set achievable goals
- Develop a support network
- Write a feelings diary
- Take time out
- Accept and like yourself
- Reduce alcohol/cigarettes
- Do relaxation/meditation
- Eat healthy and exercise
- Get plenty of sleep

This is what you need to have more of in your helium balloons

Petrol Can Analogy

I see clients regularly presenting with stress and anger. One of the reasons for this and why they struggle to manage these emotions is because they run on an empty petrol can.

If you can imagine that we all have a 'petrol can' and a 'reserve can.'   These get filled with things like food, sleep, play and relaxation. The petrol can is for your everyday life, going to work, raising a family, running the house. The reserve can is there for the unexpected. The things in life we don't plan for, such as, a death in the family, a breakdown of the car, washing machine etc, an unexpected bill, an unexpected drama.

Many people run on an empty reserve can and only half full petrol can. They can often manage this but, when they have an unexpected event, they find that they cannot cope, sometimes having periodic meltdowns and/or lashing out in anger at the people closest to them.

It is important therefore to keep your petrol can and reserve can full at all times, this means two helium balloons to every lead weight balloon.

This does not just mean keeping the petrol cans full in stressful times. It means keeping your petrol cans full at **all** times just in case the unexpected happens. None of us can predict what is around the corner.

So, managing your stress better helps you to manage your anger better,

Give you stress wings and let it fly away.

Chapter Ten
Anger Management techniques

Now that you have explored your anger, it is time to develop a plan, by developing yourself a toolbox of techniques to help you to manage your feelings. It can take some time and practice, so try to be patient and gentle with yourself as you learn these new skills. These skills become more powerful the more that you use them.

When you feel angry (energy rising) try the following:

- ✓ Try to stay calm and rational
- ✓ Think about why you are angry
- ✓ Think about who you are angry with
- ✓ Do you feel that your anger is justified?
- ✓ Decide if this anger needs to be released

If the answer is 'yes' approach the person maturely and calmly.

- ✓ Own the feeling by using "I" (I feel angry because…………)
- ✓ Try to avoid the 'you' word ("You make me angry" will put the other person on the defence)
- ✓ Use the person's behaviour rather than the person i.e.: "I'm feeling angry at the moment at these toys being left all over the floor"
- ✓ Be willing to listen to what they say back to you

This way you are releasing the anger in an effective way that:-

- ✓ The person is going to listen
- ✓ The person is going to understand what you are saying (people switch off to shouting)
- ✓ The person is less likely to lose his/her temper
- ✓ The person is more likely to negotiate
- ✓ The problem is more likely to be solved or a compromise made
- ✓ And last but not least, <u>YOU</u> will feel better, more in control and happier with the end results.

Disarming anger – dealing with people that are angry with you:

This is a useful technique when you are in a highly charged situation and you want to try and reduce feelings of anger so that you can:-

- ✓ Feel more comfortable
- ✓ Begin to listen
- ✓ Begin to start solving the problem

It is also particularly useful when someone is telling you off, or is involved in a personal tirade against you. This might be a boss, a friend, a parent or a figure of authority:

- ✓ Firstly you recognise that this person is angry towards you and respond with: *"Okay I can see that you are angry"*
- ✓ Then express your desire to solve the problem actively with: *"I want to hear and understand what you have to say"* or *"I really want us to try and work this out"*
- ✓ Get the angry person to lower their voice and to sit down, using a normal voice and calming approach: *"Let's sit down and talk about what's going on"*
- ✓ Use active listening to hear all the complaints before moving on to trying to solve the problem: *"I can see how angry that must have made you feel"*
- ✓ Whenever appropriate admit your own part in the problem: *"Yes I was being rather thoughtless/careless about that wasn't I?"* or *"I'm sorry that I made you feel that way"*

This way of approaching anger assumes you are willing to handle the problem and move beyond listening to try to resolve the conflict.

Simply placating the other person will only lead to further

conflict, especially in the long run. So, try not to sound patronising. Try to be genuine. Try to understand how the other person is feeling.

Remember that we are all different, we are all unique, and we all have different interpretations of things.

And lastly……………………………………

Taking out the heat:

When you notice yourself becoming angry, there are a number of techniques you can use to 'take the heat out' of your anger:

- ✓ Time out
- ✓ Distract yourself
- ✓ Watch a comedy
- ✓ Relaxation or meditation
- ✓ Self talk and positive thinking
- ✓ Deep breathes
- ✓ Rub the tops of your arms (self nurture)

 STOPP ACRONYM

It may be helpful to teach our clients the 'STOPP acronym' as follows:

STOP just pause for a moment

Take a breath

OBSERVE – what am I reacting to, what am I thinking and feeling? What is pushing my buttons?

PULL BACK – put in some perspective. Is there another way of looking at this? Am I misreading this situation? How important is this really?

PRACTICE – practice what works.

How to deal with your anger in a healthy way:

The constructive way of dealing with anger is to deal with it in the 'here and now' (as and when it happens) in a constructive way. Bottling it up is not managing your anger constructively.

Deal with your anger in three steps:

Feel the anger – this is to experience the anger. You may be in the habit of suppressing it, boxing it away in the back of your mind and not acknowledging this feeling and that is because it can sometimes feel uncomfortable. Find a space and some time (you don't have to respond to your feeling straight away) to acknowledge that you are feeling angry and allow yourself to feel the anger. Don't act on the emotion, which is a common thing to do.

Own the anger – be aware of what makes you angry. It is important to recognise that what makes you feel angry may not make everyone feel angry. We are all unique with different life experiences. (For example, someone who has experienced a lot of 'loss' in their lives may become extremely angry when they 'lose' something, whereas someone who has not may not feel anger at this experience at all). Therefore you need to own that this is <u>your</u> anger, linked to your uniqueness and your life experiences.

Use the anger – deal with the anger effectively, carefully, maturely and thoughtfully.

Streamline your anger:

With practice, you can streamline your anger by a technique to **"release, reduce, re-examine** and **request"** steps as follows:

1. **Release** anger physically in private. Remove yourself from the trigger situation or person. Tell significant others that you need a short break so you can think more clearly. Go somewhere safe, for a walk and swing your arms, scrub the floor, smash aluminium cans, yell into a pillow, growl, or hit a punch bag.

2. **Reduce** your anger by noticing where the tension is in your body and use the following to detach from it. Create a symbol (imagery) that represents your anger such as a firework, a volcano, a barking dog or a pan of boiling water. Focus on the symbol and watch it change. For example the firework simmer, the lava of the volcano cool, the dog stop barking or put ice cubes in the pan of hot water. If imagery does not work for you, create an acupressure point to reduce your anger, tap about 7 times the outside of the little fingernail and then tap 7 times about an inch under your collar bone. Then as you are calming further reduce your anger by moving your eyes in a horizontal figure 8 while tapping the outside points of your eyebrows. Then let the back part of your mind tackle the problem while you do something that you enjoy.

3. **Re-examine** the event that triggered your anger after detaching from it. Ask yourself 'did this incident bring up any of your own insecurities.' 'if I did not get angry, would I have felt exposed, powerless, rejected, inadequate, unimportant, guilty, ashamed, empty, bored, hungry, or tired?'   Ask yourself 'was I trying to control others?' 'Make things perfect?' 'Look tough?' 'Distance?' 'Avoid painful feelings?' 'How important is this battle?'

4. **Request** turn resentment into specific requests or action that you can take if you were truly violated. When you are

ready state your feelings, requests and solutions calmly.

Breathing Technique

Breathe slowly. Try to breathe out for longer than you breathe in and focus on each breath as you take it. **Relax** your body, if you feel your body getting tense, try focusing on each part of your body in turn to tense and then relax your muscles.

Mindfulness Techniques

Mindfulness can help you to be aware of when you are getting angry and can help calm your body and mind down. There are many mindful apps to download on mobile phones and computers to teach you mindfulness.

Exercise

Try to work off your anger through exercise. Sports like running or boxing can be really helpful for releasing pent up energy.

Use up your energy safely

This can help relieve some of your angry feelings in a way that doesn't hurt yourself or others. For example you could try tearing up a newspaper, hitting a pillow or smashing ice cubes in a sink.

Distraction techniques

Do something to distract yourself mentally or physically, anything that completely changes your situation, thoughts or patterns can help stop your anger escalating. For example putting on upbeat music and dancing, doing something with your hands like fixing something or making something creative like colouring or drawing. Write a journal or take a cold shower.

Mentally escape

Slip into a quiet room, close your eyes, and practice visualizing yourself in a relaxing scene. Focus on details in the imaginary scene. What colour is the water? How tall are the mountains? What do the chirping birds sound like? This technique can help you find calm amidst the anger.

Play some tunes

Let music carry you away from your feelings. Put in earbuds or slip out to your car. Crank up your favourite music and hum or bop your anger away.

Stop talking

When you are steamed, you may be tempted to let the angry words fly, but you are more likely to do harm than good. Pretend your lips are glued shut. This moment without speaking will give you time to collect your thoughts.

Talk to a friend

Don't stew in the events that made you angry. Help yourself process what happened by talking to a trusted, supportive friend who can help you to find a new perspective.

Laugh

Nothing upends a bad mood like a good one. Diffuse your anger by looking for ways to laugh, whether that's playing with your kids, watching stand up, or scrolling memes.

Practice gratitude

Take a moment to focus on what is right when everything feels wrong. Realising how many good things you have in life can help you neutralise anger and turn around a situation.

Write a letter

Write a letter or email to the person that made you angry. THEN DELETE IT! Often, expressing your emotions in some form is all you want and need, even if it is in something that will never be seen.

Imagine forgiving them

Finding the courage to forgive someone who has wronged you takes a lot of emotional skill. If you can't go that far, you can at least pretend that you are forgiving them, and you will feel your anger slip away.

Practice empathy

Try to walk in the other persons shoes and see the situation from their perspective. When you tell the story or relive the events as they saw it, you may gain a new understanding and become less angry.

Find a creative channel

Turn your anger into a tangible production. Consider painting, gardening or writing poetry when you are upset. Emotions are powerful muses for creative individuals. Use yours to reduce anger.

Couples that argue a lot:

Couples who are struggling with toxic arguments often have a number of harmful habits. They might yell, use personal attacks, stonewall, fail to express their feelings with words, or one of many other pitfalls. These behaviours can turn benign disagreements into heated arguments.

The **Fair Fighting Rules** handout describes the "rules of engagement" when it comes to disagreements. Instead of telling us we can't argue, fair fighting rules tell us how to do it safely and productively.

Therapists can use this handout to teach couples boundaries, warning signs, and techniques for handling disagreements. We suggest accompanying this handout with in-session practice, role-playing, and discussion of which techniques will be most helpful for a particular couple.

FAIR FIGHTING RULES

- Before you begin, ask yourself why you feel upset.

- Are you angry because your partner left the mustard on the counter? Or are you angry because you feel like you're doing an uneven share of the housework, and this is just one more piece of evidence?

- Take time to think about your own feelings before starting an argument.

- Discuss one topic at a time. Don't let "You left dishes in the sink" turn into "You watch too much TV." Discussions that get off-topic are more likely to get heated, and less likely to solve the original problem.

- Choose one topic and stick to it.

- No degrading language.

- Discuss the issue, not the person. No put-downs, swearing, or name-calling. Degrading language is an attempt to express negative feelings while making sure your partner feels just as bad. Doing so leads to more character attacks while the original issue is forgotten.

- Express your feelings with words. "I feel hurt when you ignore my phone calls." "I feel scared when you yell."

- Structure your sentences as "I" statements ("I feel emotion when event") to express how you feel while taking responsibility for your emotions. However, starting with "I" does not give a license to ignore the other fair fighting rules.

- Take turns speaking.

- Give your full attention while your partner speaks.

- Avoid making corrections or thinking about what you want to say. Your only job is to understand their point of view, even if you disagree. If you find it difficult to not interrupt, try setting a timer allowing 1-2 minutes for each person to speak without interruption.

- No stonewalling. Sometimes, the easiest way to respond to an argument is to retreat into your shell and refuse to speak. This is called stonewalling. You might feel better temporarily, but the original issue will remain unresolved and your partner will feel more upset. If you absolutely cannot go on, tell your partner that you need to take a time-out. Agree to resume the discussion later.

- No yelling. Yelling does not help anyone see your point of view. Instead, it sends the message that only your words matter. Even if yelling intimidates your partner into giving up, the underlying problem only grows worse.

- Take a time-out if things get too heated. In a perfect world, we would all follow these rules 100% of the time... but it just doesn't work like that. If an argument starts to become personal or heated, take a time-out. Agree on a time to come back and discuss the problem after everyone has cooled down.

- Attempt to come to a compromise or an understanding. There isn't always a perfect answer to an argument. Life is too messy for that. Do your best to come to a compromise (this means some give and take from both sides). If you can't come to a compromise, simply taking the time to understand your partner's perspective can help soothe negative feelings

A STORY ABOUT ANGER FOR CHILDREN & GROWNUPS INNER CHILD

Once upon a time, there was a little boy. His name was Peter. He was a very angry little boy almost all of the time. When he was angry he would hurt people, but most of all he would say very cruel things to people. Like "You smell like poo!" Or "Your hair is a frizzy mess!"

He would say spiteful and horrible things to his Mum too like "I hate you; you are the worse mum in the world." Or "You can't cook, your dinners taste of poo, you are the worst mum ever!"

Peter left everyone feeling horrible, sometimes he would make them cry. Sometimes they would not sleep at night because of the things he had said to them.

One day, his Dad had, had enough of his naughty behaviour and the hurtful things that he said to people. So, he took Peter into the garden and he said to him,

"See that fence Son, and the hammer and nails?"

"Yes" Peter replied not knowing where this was going.

"Well, every time you are horrible to someone, angry and say nasty things, you are to hammer a nail in to the fence."

"Okay," Peter said to his Dad. He was secretly pleased with such a minor punishment, that actually could be quite fun.

So every time Peter acted out his anger and hurt other people and his Mum, he went outside and hammered a nail into the fence.

Soon the fence was full of nails and there was no more room for those nails. His Dad took him outside again and said,

"Can you see all those nails in the fence Peter"

"Yes Dad" Peter replied feeling quite proud of himself.

"Well," his Dad calmly said, "Every time you are angry with someone and hurt them with words or actions you are to pull those nails out with your hands"

"Okay Dad" Peter replied, feeling angry, this was not going to be much fun at all, he thought. But, Peter was never rude or angry with his Dad, he knew better.

Peter started to remove the nails from the fence; his hands were getting more and more sore. In fact in some places, pieces of skin hung off his fingers. He cried with the pain and he struggled to sleep at night. He did not like this; he did not like it at all.

Peter became less and less angry with people and stopped saying horrible things; it was too painful pulling the nails out the fence.

One day his Dad took him outside to look at the fence again. The fence was still half filled with nails.

"You know the pain that you were in son, when you pulled those nails out of the fence with your hands"

"Yes, Dad look at my hands" he said showing his Dad his red raw hands, expecting some sympathy. "They are so sore and make me cry and stop me sleeping at night."

"Mmmm" his Dad said, hiding a smile. "That is the pain people feel when you are cruel to them in your anger and then they cry and cannot sleep at night."

"Oh, so now I get it" Peter said thinking his Dad was very clever.

"Not quite," his Dad said, leaving him to stew a little.

"Can you see the holes in the fence where you have taken the nails out Peter?" He asked.

"Yes Dad" says Peter.

"Well, Son they are the wounds that you leave behind each time you are cruel to people."

Peter hung his head in shame.

Peter was kind to people from then on. He understood the way his anger affected people, he understood their pain.

Take the 'D' out of danger and you have 'anger'

A normal emotion that is not dangerous if you respond to your anger wisely

So, control your anger or you are one letter away from Danger.

Epilogue

Thank you for buying this book. I hope that it has helped you to understand your anger better and leads you to a calmer life.

The bottom line is that anger is a normal emotion that everyone experiences from time to time. However, if you find that your anger turns to aggression or outbursts, then you need to find healthy ways to deal with anger.

If the tips, techniques, exploration and tools do not help, then maybe consider seeing a counsellor to help you to work through underlying factors that may contribute to anger and other emotional issues.

Anger is a horrid feeling to sit with; I have sat with it many times in my own life. It is more debilitating if it is anger that you feel unable to resolve. Sometimes we just have to learn to let it go. I imagine it is an unwanted salesman at my door and tell him as impolitely as possible to "Go away." Anger in itself can control your life, take over your thoughts and concentration and leave you almost chained to it, not able to do the things you want or need to do.

From the words from frozen "Let it go" – it does not help you to hang on to irresolvable anger. I will leave you with another story

THE RUNAWAY PALACE

Long, long ago when the world was so full of magic that even the smallest stone could hold a thousand secrets, there was a palace that was alive. Because it slept all the time, nobody knew its secret.

It remained that way until the Princess who lived there married a Prince who was a brave and strong warrior but, had such a bad temper that even the smallest inconvenience would cause him to hurl things around and slam doors and windows.

After his last victory, he let the kind and sweet Princess leave the palace to travel and negotiate the peace, leaving the Prince alone for a long time.

The Prince's boredom caused his bad temper to grow worse and with the passing days, more and more marks and dents appeared on the walls and floors of the palace, which grew dirty and neglected.

One day, when the Prince went out, the palace, annoyed at how it was being treated, woke up and moved for the first time in many years. It decided to hide behind a hill, but was so big that it didn't take too long for the Prince to find it again.

The palace tried to escape many times but the Prince would always find it easily and he would then unleash his fury, causing more and more damage. One night, having grown tired of the Prince's actions, the palace locked its doors and windows while the Prince slept. The palace ran for days and says, ignoring the damage and destruction the Prince was causing while trapped inside.

When the palace finally stopped and opened its doors, the Prince discovered that they were surrounded by ice and snow, in the midst of the most horrible cold.

"We are in the North Pole. How do I get out of here?" wondered the Prince as he explored his new surroundings.

After searching all morning and finding nothing, the Prince decided to go back to the palace to warm up. However, when he tried to open the door he found it locked. He banged on the door furiously but all he managed to do was destroy his near-frozen hands. After a while, the door opened slightly and the Prince ran towards it, only for it to slam in his face.

"Stupid Palace! It seems angry with me!"

The palace was indeed angry with the Prince and shook all its windows to let him know.

"So that's the way you want it!" shouted the Prince. "well get ready, because this is war and I have never lost a battle!"

In the days that followed, the Prince and the palace had the strangest fight imaginable. While the Prince tried to get in by breaking the windows, the palace did whatever it could to keep him out.

In the middle of that crazy war, the cold began to freeze the Prince's feet and crack the palace walls. When he was almost completely frozen solid the Prince, winner of a thousand battles, realised that the only way to win this one would be to make peace. So the Prince began to repair the palace and to control his anger and fury so as not to damage it again.

The palace soon realised that it liked the repairs much more than the stupid fighting and that only that brutish Prince could do them. Soon enough, the palace opened its doors to allow the Prince to shelter from the cold at night and clean and repair by day.

Much to his surprise, the Prince discovered that he really enjoyed doing the repairs and in no time the palace looked magnificent once again. So much so, that one night it finally forgave the Prince, closed its doors and ran all the way back to its country. They arrived just before the Princess, who was delighted with the state of the palace and the peace improved character of her husband, now barely interested in wars and fighting any more.

The lasting peace and the Princes repairs meant the palace could finally resume its silent sleep. The only thing anyone knows about this unique palace is that it was taken down stone by stone and distributed around the world. Some of the stones could well be part of your house today, so don't let anger and temper cause it any damage.........................

Remember one minute of anger loses you sixty seconds of happiness.

Other books by this Author

OTHER BOOKS BY THIS AUTHOR:

Novels:
Gut Instinct
Jane, me and myself
The Haymaker
Woman's World
She is my mum too
Megan's Choice (Coming soon 2021)
FOLIE A DEUX (Coming soon 2021)

Self help books:
I shall wear purple
I shall be blue
I shall be clean
I shall be calm
I shall be cool
I shall be free (Coming soon 2021)
Me, Me, Me - An inside look into the fragile heart
of a self absorbed mother
Teenagers are from Pluto

Children's books:
The Fairy on top of the Christmas tree
The Mystery behind Grandpa's Chair
Crystal Magic
Friends in the rainforest
Have no fear a dinosaur is here

Text Books
Introduction to counselling theory and skills
Training manual for counselling for certificate to diploma in therapeutic
counselling
Counselling and Psychotherapy Training Level 4 & 5

"I knew I was an unwanted baby when I saw my bath toys were a toaster and a radio." I've never forgotten that quote. I like quotes. I enjoy the mystery behind them. I take pleasure in the riddle and sometimes confusion that they might cause. But best of all I have a weakness for the way that they play with people's minds and the diverse interpretations that can be seen in them. They can become our secrets that we conceal from others. We can hide how we really feel in a quote by developing our own interpretation and keeping that interpretation to ourselves. We can pretend that it is humour rather than reveal that it is reality. They can express how we are really feeling as well as say a mountain of things in one powerful short sentence.

I was an unwanted baby I knew that from the minute that I was born. I'd read this quote in one of my mother's magazines, when I was a child. It was cited by Joan Rivers. I had spent hours and hours admiring her camera-friendly face. The large eyes that glared out at me from the glossy page seemed to follow me which ever direction I moved to. I believed at the time that this was what I should look like, be like. That I too could make a joke about my horrific childhood and that this in itself would take away my psychological pain.

I was around thirteen years of age, when I came across Joan Rivers. She had the same kind of mother as I had. I had no longer felt so alone in the world, knowing that there were others out there just like me, who had achieved success. Who were able to one day escape and put the horror behind them and do something special with their lives. Turn their wounds into wisdom. One day I will be famous I had thought, and I will say things like that. I will let them know exactly what my mother was – a whore, a child abuser and a nonentity. Or at least she was now.

I'd had vivid dreams, colourful imaginings that never came true, thoughts of happiness and contentment, love and peace. It was my life, and my waking hours that had been one long gruesome nightmare. My sleep had been my respite where I could wish for happier times, when I could dream about blissful times, about becoming someone like the flamboyant and humorous Joan Rivers. Those dreams in my childhood are what had kept me sane. They had kept me from wanting to die. They gave me something to live for, to hope for. When I awoke I would want to sleep again, to go back into the reverie that helped me to escape my wretched life. My whole days were spent praying for the end of the day, wishing my days away so that I could relax and feel safe, for the few hours of sleep that I was able to get.

Being born is like a lottery, you don't know which mother you are going to get. You stand helplessly in the queue hoping and praying that the woman that would look endearingly into your eyes, whilst still feeling moist from the long and painful journey down the birth canal would be a loving and kind person. You hoped that the woman *whose arms that you lay in would smell of sweet soap and cleanliness and not stale cigarettes, alcohol and body odour.*

I was number 326. I was lining up waiting to be embedded in some woman's womb. Ironically 325 didn't feel well on the day of my consummation so he was made to sit out. If he had been well, then my life might have been so very different. I would have had a nice mother then. Instead I got 'her'. Instead I drew the short straw.

Did your child draw the short straw?

Hey you! I'm talking to you!

Put the book down,

YES YOU!

The lottery of life, the lottery of parentage is the luck of the draw.

Furthermore, did your child get the short straw? Or was she or he the lucky one who won the lottery! Have you created a monster, look at your child? Have you made him who he is today   due to your own narcissistic personality, your own internal madness? Have you inflicted this horror on to your child?

"We are not makers of history. We are made by our history" by Martin Luther King Junior is another quotation which is a particular favourite of mine.

If this is the case, this means that I have been made by my history, my life has made me who I am. My mother, she has made me who I am today. Or would I have been like this anyway, was it in my DNA, was it nature or nurture? Perhaps you will be able to answer my question after reading my story, after living in my world even if just for the time it takes to read this book, or after stepping into the shoes that I was forced to wear either by my upbringing or by my DNA.

Everything I do is justified; I have a calling to save the world from mothers like mine.

Do you admire my strength of character or do you despise me? Please don't judge me as you read my story as this could have been you! If you had drawn the short straw just like I did.

I had a path to take and I took it. Some devious people decided to place 'socio' in front of it.

Reviews for "Gut Instinct"

Mather has created an exciting and fast paced thrill ride.

Her characters are sympathetic and believable. She adds several twists to keep the reader turning the page. As a mystery writer myself, I expect a good deal from an author in this genre. Mather delivers. Because of her professional background, Mather is a master of the Psychological Thriller.

Her keen insight into human nature and her ability to surprise the reader, make this novel a must read for mystery fans. I look forward to more works from this first time novelist.

Ali Roberti - Author of NEVERMORE

Brilliant!!!,

I was engrossed right from the start. Excellent piece of writing, keeps you hanging on the whole way through! I love psychological thrillers; this is one of the best I have read in a long time! What an ending, well done, the author fantastic read!!!!

Twisted tale!
I was sucked into the story early on and spent the rest of the day reading. Easy to read, amusing, puzzling, sad, savage, insightful AND with a twist in the tale. I am looking forward to the next book.

Brilliant
Well I didn't expect that at the end. I couldn't put this book down and read 30 chapters in one night. Well done on a brilliant book.

Excellent!
This is an excellent read, the author has the style of James Patterson and although a slow beginning a page turner four chapters in.

Brilliant Read!
I could not put this book down it should be turned into a film. What an ending!!!

Mindboggling!
This book is an incredible psychological thriller that has you gripped from beginning to end, and what an ending. This author is a wonderful storyteller. I would recommend it to anyone who likes thrillers to read this

Great book!
I read this book in two days, considering if I can't get into a book within the first two chapters I don't read it, I would say that it says a lot for this book. Very well written, good story. Would recommend it. Well done Linda Mather. I can't wait to read the next one going to download it now.

I'm a qualified psychotherapist. I wanted to help people. No I need to start by being honest. The truth is I needed to save myself. This is why I did the training. I was what psychotherapy trainers call 'a client in disguise'.

I grew up living in fear, living in fight or flight all of the time. I never quite learned how to relax and just be 'me' and who I was meant to be. One minute I was a people pleaser trying to keep myself safe, the next I was a rebel, fighting to stay safe, whenever I felt at risk.

Now, I don't know who I am. My existence I believe was purely to support three clients. I did what I had to do; one of those clients is living a good life now, and the other two? Well you will read what happened to the other two. They vanished off the face of the earth, Like me, they sacrificed their lives for another. Do I regret it? No I did what I had to do. It is what it is. Was my work unethical, was it dangerous? Some would say it was, some would say I took an incredible risk I will leave you the reader to decide on that.

People think psychotherapy is to just sit with the client and listen, a dumping ground for all the client's problems. It is, yes, a sharing of those problems of course, but from my experience it is much more than that. It is helping the client to understand why they maybe have these problems. What have they experienced in their lives that impact on them now. The question that we always wonder is 'what happened to you?' How did you get here? Psychotherapy is partly exploring the emotional effects of psychological wounds on children and how they manifest themselves later in adults. This is my story, how I worked with the wounds of my three clients, alongside working with my own psychological wounds too.

It all began when I was newly qualified to work predominantly with people's emotional wellbeing. However, I was lucky enough to be referred a client that has quite serious mental health problems but only if there is an evidence base that psychotherapy has had positive results in the past with the presenting issue. Everything we do these days have to be evidence based, which is if you ask me a pain in the backside. I, and many others believe that the 'relationship' between client and counsellor is the most powerful tool, this can be hard to measure. How do you measure the relationship that helps the client to reach understanding, healing and change? It may not be Cognitive behavioural therapy, or person centred therapy or psychodynamic that has helped to cure a client's depression, but that of the relationship between the therapist and the client. This can by no means be researched or evaluated, that is because we are two human beings with our own special way of relating.

I enjoy the challenge of this work, because the complexity of the human mind and mental health issues has always interested me. I enjoy the relationship that develops between me and my clients and that is my focus rather than bombarding the client with homework tools, or analytical jargon.

It takes time to build the relationship, to build the trust that is paramount to the therapeutic relationship.   It takes as long as it takes with each individual client, to develop an intimacy which requires the repeated experience of being responded to. This does not happen with theory or therapeutic models of therapy, they are just interventions to support the relationship. Without the relationship therapeutic tools do not work. That is from my experience, both as a therapist and as a client.

I absolutely love my work, I love the diverse people that I get to meet and I love to observe the emotional growth that I see with my clients. Although it would be unethical for me to see my clients for personal reward, it would be a lie to say that I didn't feel a sense of satisfaction, when a client ended therapy in a much better place than when they started. I enjoy supporting my clients to reach their long term goals. It is an uplifting experience when I see their stuckness unravel before my eyes, like a ball of tangled wool, or when that light bulb experience brightly lights up the therapy room. I love to watch silently the facial expression of the client who comes to some life changing awareness.

I love that I learn as much from them as they learn from me. It gives me a great sense of fulfilment, when each client that I work with helps me to grow, not only as a professional but as a person too.

Psychotherapy is as much about the relationship as it is about the skills and the theory. Developing an intimate relationship with my clients where they feel safe enough to share concerns or histories that they have never shared with anyone else, or that they have shared and received uninterested or negative responses is a gratifying part of the job. To gain an understanding of their experience and help them to heal their own pain is awe inspiring. It doesn't feel for me like a job, it feels like a vocation that I would have done for free rather than not do at all. All I ever wanted was to be able to hold the space, emotionally connect and reach out and touch another human being with my heart. I believe I succeeded in doing this.

The story that I am about to tell you is concerning three clients, whom during our sometimes dramatic and traumatic time together, tested both my professionalism and my strength. They caused me to question my moral and ethical principles and they weathered my own emotions at the same time colliding with feelings of great joy. It is a heartbreaking story that I have no doubt will shock you to the core. It will command you to examine the complexity of the human mind. It will make you question my motives and wander what the hell I was doing at times.

It is a story that will test your strength to its limits, and it will without any doubt pull on your heart strings so violently, that is may leave you in floods of tears. It is okay to cry this means that you are most likely an empath.   Empath's are highly sensitive people who are too often perceived as weaklings. To feel intensely is not a symptom of weakness; it is the trademark of the truly alive and compassionate. It is not the empath that is broken; it is society that has become dysfunctional and emotionally disabled. Those who are at times described as being a 'hot mess' are the fabric of what keeps the dream alive for a more caring, humane world. I am a hot mess, most of the time and for me that is okay.

This story, my story is also a heart warming story that examines human emotions and the capacity of pain in which one human being is able to endure. I know with certainty that even after reading this unusual but honest account, Jane, Jack and Jasmine will linger in your thoughts long after you put the book down.

All three of my charming but intricate clients accessed my services at around the same time. It was in May 2010, just when spring was ready to encounter summer and for me the best time of the year. It is the time when the daffodils are out in bloom providing a ray of colour in the once bleak gardens. The summer flowers are just beginning to shyly steal a look at the world as they peer through the damp soil. It is when the fragrant smell of flowers and crisp air ventilates the house, as the curtains sway in the subtle breeze pouring through the now open windows. It is a season that energises people into new beginnings, a time for growth and change for both nature and for people.   It is a comfortable and endurable time where we are not shivering in the freezing cold of winter or sweltering in the blistering heat of summer.

I have worked tirelessly with these clients for just over three years, through twelve spectacular changes of the seasons. Each season bringing new revelations and resurrecting new emotions, emotions for all of us that we had never before experienced. Stepping into all of their worlds was overwhelmingly painful. Stepping out was the beginning of my end, an excruciating and painful conclusion to a therapeutic journey that was to end my career. I experienced loss how no other person has, and will possibly never do again. I lost 'me' and all that I stood for, all that I worked for. I lost who I was, who I had worked hard to be, to give one of my clients the freedom to live.

In the beginning a good many long hours were spent building up relationships with Jack, Jane and Jasmine whom all predictably had trust issues. These needed to be assiduously worked through before the fundamental work could begin. It was a difficult and painful passage of time, where we shared tears of sadness and tears of joy and we faced many challenges as the seasons continued to transform and unfold. It was a period of painful endings and a cycle of apprehensive new beginnings, for all of us. It was an interval of my life that I will never forget.

Reviews for 'Jane Me and Myself'

Brilliant

This is an amazing book reflecting the complexity of DID.

It is written with compassion and also excellent factual insight. At the end I cried   which says a lot as it takes real talent to move me to tears with a fiction book. Having experienced trauma myself I found myself identifying with many points,
Page turner for Me, Myself and I

I shall be cool

Well, I couldn't put this book down. What a fantastic read. I am now looking for more books to read with this talented author. Read this especially if you find psychological influences in our minds fascinating. Wow never a slow page. I will enjoy this book over and over.

Fantastic Read

I am studying to be a counsellor myself and this book was just fantastic. Some of this book will help me with my studies and my work when I become a counsellor myself. I loved the twists and turns that came along during reading this book. I do hope that the author writes more books like this one and Gut Instinct. Both books are very hard to put down once you start reading them. Tell the housework it can wait while you sit and enjoy these two books.

Sad but very good

What a fabulous book! Sad but very good. I didn't see the twist in the tale coming, It is one of those books you cannot put down.

Jane, Me and Myself

I found this book to be very thought provoking and riveting. I could not put this book down, it was a real page turner and not for one minute did I see the mysterious twist at the very end!

Gripping

Absolutely amazing. I was gripped from the very start.

Thought provoking

A very good read. I didn't see the twist coming at all, Thank you for such a poignant story about mental health issues.

Five stars

Love it, what more can I say.

I shall be cool

My narrative is one that you will find hard to believe particularly if by the time you read my story we are still fortunate enough to be living in a world of equality between men and women. A world where both sexes have an input into the way our country is run, where no one gender has all the power, where men are not deemed as a second rate citizen. It has not always been like this, as you will read. I lived in a world that was unkind, unfair and painful.

I am an historian and I have written this book in the hope that it will be read by many people in years to come and will deter people from believing that a world where one sex has more power than another is a functional civilization. On the contrary a world ruled and manipulated by one gender is as I experienced to be a dysfunctional society.

It is not a healthy society and is not I believe a culture that we were made to live in. We were made to live together as men and women equally. We were made to love.

The world as it is today is far, far different from the world that I grew up in and the world that I risked my life to fight for. I hope that you appreciate mine and many other courageous freedom fighters efforts in giving you the freedom that you now enjoy.

This is my story.

The underground room holding the weekly E.R.P.M meetings were always full with enthusiastic supporters. Excited freedom fighters eager to change the way that the United Kingdom and as far as we knew at the time the world was now being run. For these meetings we surreptitiously used a large room in a derelict underground station, which was at this time out of use.

All the underground stations were abandoned and boarded up in these days, cold and damp and void of the industrious activity that once was. Where shoppers and workers dashed around trying to reach their destination, jumping aboard high speed trains before their automatic doors closed, the whoosh of air breaks alerting people that it was coming to a halt. There would have been voices over speakers announcing stops, as people pushed and shoved to ensure they were able to aboard.

These stations and trains were far too often targeted for terrorist attacks because of the high casualty numbers and the ability to destroy a means of transportation for so many people, the terrorists hoping not only to create widespread fear but also to shut down cities.

These stations had been closed and left to rot countrywide since the monorail system was built in 2025. Now we fly through the sky looking down at the buildings below, reminiscent of a miniature town.

I shall be cool

The room that we used may have once been a large cafeteria, a waiting room or maybe even a newsagent in its time. It was now a meeting room for 'the organisation' which was what we called our group to protect its true identity. The meetings were underground in more than one sense and they were organised with the highest level of secrecy.

It was the year 2044 and we were now almost twenty years into what the government relished in calling 'the new world.' - A Woman's world.

The country at this time had its third female prime minister, who had been elected to power for the previous twenty years. In the past this role had been primarily a man's role prior to and since the late 1970's when we were governed by a strong, no nonsense woman named Margaret Thatcher, the very first female prime minister.

Margaret Thatcher made many changes to the country and many people from this generation would say for the worse. She was described as a cold distant woman whom took the country to war with the Falklands.

If you were lucky enough to find and spend the time speaking with the men who tirelessly worked the now closed and dilapidated coalmines in England and Wales, they would happily reel off stories of how she was the start of the destruction of the coalmining industry in this country. The coalmining industry was replaced by fracking in 2015 which was an advanced technology of extraction of shale gas as a way of bridging the gap between fossil fuels and low carbon energy. However, this was stopped in 2025 due to the significant impact that it had on our countryside, wildlife and climate, leaving the country for a brief while short of fuel and leaving us in the dark in more ways than one, with regular power cuts due to the shortage of energy.

This was a huge mistake by the politicians of this time who appeared to have very limited foresight into the impact of their decisions.

The second female prime minister was Theresa May, she was prime minister from 2016 to 2019. As prime minister she began the process of withdrawing the UK from the European union and was a big part of the brexit negotiations, however she could not get her party to agree a fair deal, people described her as a weak leader of her party, and in 2019 she resigned.

Since then no female was elected as prime minister until 2024. Theresa May left a fear in the country of ever voting a female to lead this country for nearly ten years.

The crown was also held by a female. The Queen was the first daughter of King William. Up until 2012 the heir to the throne was always the first born son to the King and Queen, unless they didn't bear any sons, of course. Since 2012 it was decided that the heir to the throne would go to the crowns first born child immaterial of what sex the heir was. In the event that the monarch had multiple births, the heir to the throne would be the first baby delivered. William's first born was in fact a boy but, the in this new world the crown always went to a woman. The throne went to Princess Charlotte.

Queen Charlotte the new heir to the throne, like all of us women of this time, was not allowed to marry, so therefore had no consort as such, her escort was always her lady in waiting. Rumour had it that their relationship was intimate, but there were always rumours about the Queen and no doubt always would be because unlike over twenty years ago the media were not allowed to publish anything about the royal family, unless approved by the royal family or 'the firm' as it was sometimes called.

It had taken twenty years after the death of Princess Diana, William and his brother Prince Harry's mother for 'the firm' and the government to enforce this rule, even though Diana was hounded by the press and eventually died in an horrific car crash after being chased by the media in an underground tunnel in Paris.   Prince Harry had fought for decades for the royal family to have some level of privacy in the wake of his mother's death.

Unlike many, I knew all of this information because I was one of the privileged few to be able to study history at school. Very few could do this and particularly none of the boys. The government did not want males to get any ideas above their station. They didn't want a crusade on their hands. Men were second class citizens in this era and the education system suppressed their right to knowledge from a very young age.

To study this subject I had to sign a contract at the time swearing me to secrecy to prevent me from sharing historical knowledge with anyone else. The government was very protective of our history and only a select few would be privy to this information. The rationale behind this I believe is so that the people believed that the way we lived now was the best way, the only way that we should live.

The reason that I was lucky enough to have had the freedom to study this very interesting subject at school was that I had chosen to work in research for the government. I, like most of us girls and boys, were forced to choose our career path at fourteen and unless we had medical grounds for this to be changed at a later date, that was what we had to do. The boys however, were only allowed to study manual subjects such as gardening, engineering, carpentry, bricklaying etc. The girls had what the government deemed to be the more academic jobs or national or public services roles to choose from if they wished.

I chose research because even at that young age I was curious about our roots and unhappy with how the world was. I wanted to make changes for the better. I wanted the world to live in equality and in peace and I felt that other than a job in politics which was for the elite of our society, that this would get me nearer to my goal. This would get my foot in the door. I wanted to make a difference. I wanted change.

I attended these clandestine meetings to do just that to make a difference, even though if any of us were caught, there would be dire consequences. I would lose my job, my home and spend the rest of my life 'working for the government' but this time in an institution.   I would lose what little freedom I had. That would be the consequences of our betrayal. This was a risk that I was prepared to take, for society, for my future children that I was adamant I would have and for their children.

This was why I steadfastly became a freedom fighter for a cause I stealthily supported.

Reviews for "A woman's world
A thought provoking book.

Another great book! This author has the ability to get you thinking even after you have finished the book.

Food for thought

Would the grass be greener? Would the world be a better place? This is a story that gives us insights into the alternatives and asks us 'Which world would you prefer to live in?' Linda's second novel is as easy to read as the first and just as enjoyable. I suspect the film would have plenty of scope for some interesting details.

Good Storyteller

I am impressed with your story telling abilities.

Thought provoking

This is an interesting concept; this writer has a good way of telling stories, a thought provoking book. A thoroughly enjoyable read.

My earliest recollection of being 'different' from other people was when I was five years old. I wasn't interested in playing the 'silly' games that they played at nursery school. I had felt old, beyond my years. I was easily bored by the simplification of Fairy tales or Peter and Jane books. I wasn't interested in anything other than general knowledge and listening to stories from the bible, historical events or stories based on true facts.

I was a very supportive class mate and would be the first on the scene if someone was hurt or crying. I fascinated my teachers and my family by how empathic I was at such a young age when most children of this age appear to be more self-absorbed. They commented on how quickly that I could calm a child down, even those that were older than I was. As I went through my school days I became well known among my peers as the student counsellor, listening to everyone's stories and solving everyone's problems.

At fourteen years of age I was awarded 'The Princess Diana award' for my achievements at school and for the help and support given to my peers. It was an honour to receive this amazing award but at the same time I did not like the attention that this brought to me. I was a quiet boy and I was not comfortable to be the centre of attention. I liked it best when I could dissolve into the background, unnoticed and insignificant. My mother however was the opposite. She enthusiastically basked in the attention and the compliments on what a fine son she had raised, which she received from my teachers and the other parents. I didn't mind she deserved it. She had done a fine job, she had raised me on her own.

I was around ten years old when I asked my mother who my father was. She told me that I didn't have a father and I believed her. I believed her story that I was a gift to her from God and this fit in with what 'the lady in white' had told me. I need to make you aware at this point that my mother is a wonderful, loving and nurturing woman who has dedicated her life to me. My childhood was a happy one. We were very close and she would always proudly say how 'in-tune' we were with each other and we were. Sometimes she would even know what I was thinking. I used to believe that she was magical. I later believed this to be down to a 'mother's natural instinct'.

I became appreciably aware of my 'gift' at about the age of six or seven when I found a small frightened bird in my garden. It had a broken wing. It lay on the ground looking defeated as if ready to die. I made the bird a nest in a shoe box and gently lay it inside. I nurtured it back to health. Well that is what everyone else thought. The truth is that the bird's wing healed the minute that I put my hand on it. I watched in awe as the bird's skin sculpted together again and the feathers spread over the newly formed skin. The bird looked up into my eyes knowingly as if thanking me for healing it. It ravenously tucked into the bread and milk that I had made. A day later it flew into the blue cloudless sky never to be seen again.

I shall be cool

The second time this happened was when I was about eight or nine. My friend Robert fell off his bike. He rolled around the ground screeching in pain holding his shin with both hands. When I managed to remove his hands from the bloody wound, there was a four inch gash about four millimetres deep. It would need stitches I had thought. I gently lay my hand over the wound to stop the bleeding, when I removed my hand to my amazement there was just a slight graze. Luckily Robert did not see the original injury or he would undoubtedly have been freaked out. Instead he was embarrassed about the fuss he had made over such a small injury.

It was then that I came to the realisation that I had some sort of healing powers, but I never for one minute thought of the impact that this would later have on my life. It never crossed my mind that it was so unique. It never occurred to me that this gift would later become such a burden. To be honest, I don't really remember what I thought at the time as we just carried on happily with our bike ride. The only thing I did know was that I must keep it a secret. How I knew this I will never know, but I told no-one, not even my mother, for several years. In hindsight I wish I had kept it my secret for life.

It was the same when at nine years old I had the most amazing vision. I was alone in the house. My mother had nipped to my adopted Grandmother's house two streets away as she had been ill and needed her help. I had just stepped out of the bath and had put on my pyjamas obediently following my mother's instructions before she had left. She had promised that we would watch a DVD when she returned and I was looking forward to this. It was the new movie Les Miserable and unlike most children my age I loved musicals and musical theatre.

Suddenly the light bulb in my bedroom flickered and went out. I thought the bulb had blown and as I turned around to go get a new one out of the kitchen cupboards, I noticed my room light up, almost like a torch blindingly shining in my face and at the same time there was a great sound of a trumpet.   It was then that I saw her.

She stood in the corner of my room. She was a beautiful angelic figure dressed in white. I looked for her wings, but she had no wings, so I immediately doubted that she was an angel sent from heaven.   Never the less I knew that she was someone extraordinary, someone that only I would see. She asked me in a gentle melodic voice not to be scared. She told me the story of exactly who I was and whom I was related to. I sat mesmerised at this beautiful woman's story.

Then as quickly as she came she disappeared giving me no time to ask any questions. The bulb on my bedside lamp came to life again and I stood for few seconds wondering if I had dreamt the whole thing. Although I knew deep down that I hadn't. I was overjoyed and felt very honoured to find that my ancestry was so very important.

It was that night that my mother came home and told me that my adopted Grandmother had died. I will now tell you my story, it is an honest account and completely true.

I shall be cool

My story began on 28th October 1958 in a small bedroom at the back of my paternal grandparents two up, two down house. The midwife had arrived at the house on her old, squeaky bicycle having been notified that my mum was in labour. Mum delivered me naturally without the aid of pain relief. She had just a pillow to bite on, which the midwife had given to her on becoming aware that my grandmother and two neighbours were pryingly listening at the door. They had covered the budgerigar's cage to silence it so that they could hear the sound of the baby's first cries or as my mum believed they could hear her moans of pain.   This meant that my brave and poor mum had to suffer in silence and ironically was what both she and I continued to do for the rest of our lives. My birth father was down the pub either for a pre birth celebration or because he didn't give a damn about either of us, which given his personality and subsequent acts I would guess it to be the later.

Mum was a vivacious, beautiful and loving mother; she had the look of Elizabeth Taylor with her jet black, back combed hair and her ruby red lips. She was married to a serious domestic violent man who would often beat her to a pulp. She suffered broken ribs, black eyes and many other serious injuries. He would think nothing of the bruises he administered to her porcelain skin, which she would then cover by gently applying make-up, her tough cookie mask and a smile to avoid the meddlesome neighbours gossiping, or offering meaningful sympathy.

We lived in a small mining village in Easington Colliery, County Durham, where everyone knew everyone; old housewives in polka dot aprons, would talk over the garden fence, curlers forever in their hair, spreading gossip from one end of the village to the other. By the time the kettle had boiled for their fresh cup of tea the gossip would have amplified and become something of a mountain rather than the molehill it possibly was. It was similar to the modern day facebook of spreading information speedily and animatedly across the village and thankfully not across the world, soon to be forgotten by the next piece of juicy scandal to come along, busy bodies that focused on other people's glass houses, rather than their own. It was a way of life, it was a way of vamping up their lives whilst their husbands were busy working down the mines or at the local club or pub for a pint.

Mum was one of seven children. She was the third child and the eldest daughter of a coal miner and a housekeeping mother. Mums, Great Granddad Owen Burns and Great Grandma, Mary Burns came over to England from Ireland in the 1850's, with mums Granddad, James Burns as well as his brother and sister when they were still children. We therefore have Irish ancestors which does not surprise me in the least, it accounts for mums fun loving and lively personality. Our ancestors left Ireland and settled in a town called Hetton Downs in County Durham. It is coincidental that we took

Mum and Dad to Dublin in Ireland for their 40th wedding anniversary, unaware that we were taking mum back to her very early roots.

Irelands population fell from more than 8 million to just 6.5 million between 1841 and 1851. A century later it had dropped to 4.3 million due to the emigration of families to England. Some of this movement was temporary made up of seasonal harvest labourers working in Britain and returning home for winter and spring. Some was to escape the ongoing sectarian violence and its economic aftermath being a major factor for immigration. Britain's wartime economy and post war boom attracted many Irish people to expanding cities and towns. Irish immigration to Britain followed the pattern of industrialisation. Although there were periods and areas of resistance to their arrival, the Irish found it relatively easy to find work, mainly because they were willing to take on gruelling work, often in harsh environments. While the work was hard and low skilled, it was not necessarily poorly paid.

In the north east of England concentrations of the Irish formed in the dockland areas of Newcastle and Tynemouth and along the south bank of the Tyne, with a wide scattering in the furnace towns and pit villages of County Durham and this is where it appears my ancestors settled, all being coal miners for the generations to come.

My Great Grandfather was looked after and worked for a family named Ivers. He met and fell in love with a servant of the house Mary Ellen Kelly who's brothers were miners and also boarding with the Ivers. They eventually married and had children one being my Granddad who they named after the man that took them both in and was exceptionally kind to them. My maternal Grandfathers name was John Ivers Burns (Jack). My Great Grandfather died in 1907 aged 43. His wife was a widow at 41 and went on to remarry a man named Laws.

My maternal Grandmother was born in 1910 after her parents had lost a child aged 1. The child's name was Elizabeth Violet Cumming. They named my Grandmother Violet Cumming after this child and she was to be one of nine children. Living with the name of her deceased sister was a hard act to follow, as well as being nurtured by parents who must have been beside themselves with grief.

Elizabeth was not the only child to die at a young age in this family. My Grandmothers brother was a private in the Yorkshire light infantry who was killed in action aged 15 in August 1918 and is buried in Flanders Field in France, with many other soldiers whom died in this battle.

Flanders is a region in Belgium, the name deriving from a medieval state that encompassed parts of what are now Belgium and Northern France. However, the soldiers in the First World War would often refer to their service on the Western Front as "France", whether it was in France itself or Belgium. The principal town around which the fighting in Flanders revolved was Ypres, and the area around the town of Ypres was also known as the Salient. This region was fought over from October 1914 until practically the end of the war in November 1918.

My great uncle Stephen Cumming bravely fought in the third battle of Ypres, in the Flanders region of Belgium where the German army launched one of the first chemical attacks in the history of war.

I shall be cool

John McCrae who fought in the second battle of Ypres wrote the following poem, which is still recited on Remembrance Sunday now and is where the idea of Poppies originated to remember the men who lost their lives in battle:

In Flanders fields the poppies blow,
Between the crosses row on row,
That mark our place and in the sky
The larks still bravely singing, fly.
Scarce heard amid the guns below,
We are the dead, short days ago,
We lived, felt dawn, saw sunset glow
Loved and were loved and now we lie in Flanders fields
Take up our quarrel with the foe
To you from falling hands we throw
The torch be yours to hold it high
If ye break faith with us who die
We shall not sleep, though poppies grow in Flanders fields.

This is part of my history, sadly my brothers felt the need to take away my history in the end by the way they acted refusing me memorabilia from my parents house, photographs etc. They couldn't and they never will because I have my history given to me by my parents long before they died. This is indeed my brother's history too.

Granddad and Grandma Burns met and married in 1930 and went on to have 7 children, 4 boys and 3 girls. Life was not great for mum growing up as both of her parents had a volatile relationship, and as for most in those days money was tight. Some of mum's early childhood was throughout the Second World War, and the post war years, where there were rations on food and sometimes daily air raid sirens blasting through the streets. Fathers and brothers were sent to war with no knowing if they would come home or not. Home for mum during some of that time was divided between the small three bedroom family home, where the children slept top to tail in their beds and the bomb shelter, where they would be woken up from their sleep and rushed to shelter from the German bombs, which destroyed many cities and towns.

During WW2 coal miners were not required for call up to armed service - their job was digging the then main source of energy here in the UK 'coal'. Never the less this did not ensure my Grandfather's safety as he would refuse to go to the bomb shelter when the air raid sirens went off, instead staying at home sitting under the large family dining table alone. My grandmother with her children clinging on to her apron strings would make her way back home after the bombing had ceased and not know if their father, her husband would be alive or dead. Fortunately he was always safe and well.

My Grandmother was Salvation Army, later to convert to catholic when she married my Grandfather who was a Roman Catholic. As an adult he did not attend church himself but he would send his children to church every week and on their return ask them to preach the priest's sermon that day, so that he knew they had attended.

The children soon learned how to trick their father and each week one of them would go to church while the others would go down to Easington Beach and play. They would meet up again a couple of hours later and the child whose turn it was to go to church would tell the others what the sermon had been about on that particular Sunday so that they could recite it back to their Father on their return. He never knew of their clever trick, and all the children would remember and recite this story to us children as we grew up. One child would come home smelling of tapestry and candles and the others of sea salt and sand, but their father never seemed to notice, and a good job too as punishment in those days would be their backsides whipped with his belt.

It was on one of these trips to the beach that mum nearly drowned. The kids had been so engrossed in their game for several hours they had not noticed that the tide had come in. When it was time to return home they saw that they were now on an island surrounded by sea so in panic and fear they had to swim to shore. Mum couldn't swim so although the others helped her she slipped under the water several times, coming up to the surface gasping for breath. This gave her a fear of water and therefore a fear of learning to swim for all of her life.

They were a poor family but reasonably happy, spending long summer nights playing on the streets that were much safer in those days, the girls chalking up squares for hop scotch and the boys playing cricket using a dustbin lid as a wicket. Neighbours would pop in borrowing cups of sugar, passing on the local gossip, whilst sipping endless cups of sweet tea, keeping as close an eye on their baking stottie cakes as they did their boisterous children. Mum's rarely went to work, they spent their days beating dusty sometimes threadbare carpets outside on the washing lines and washing clothes by hand to the aroma of baking bread cooking on the oven heated at the side of the coal burning fire.

The kitchen was part of the living room, the focal point of the house where everyday living took place. There was a small pantry which incorporated a sink with room for only the person allocated to do the washing up. This is where the very sparse food was stored. The pantry was also in my times with my Grandmother a shelter that we would huddle up in, during thunder storms. Gran, I and a whippet dog named Vicky (who was twice the size she should have been due to Gran incessantly feeding her with kit kats). When lightning was to strike, all the silver was hidden in drawers and cupboards to not attract a lightning strike (she said). We would sometimes sit in the pantry for hours, the dogs arse in my face whilst Gran told me fairy stories of princes, princesses, dragons and wicked stepmothers, me periodically pinching my nose when the dog let off a smelly fart. I would have rather faced the thunderstorm, then spend hours with a farting dog in a small enclosed space.

As difficult as mums times were as a child she would often describe them as happy times as well as sad. With seven boisterous children, 4 boys and 3 girls there was plenty of noise and laughter in the house. The only thing that marred that happiness was their parent's very vocal and sometimes physical rows. Mum could recall several occasions where her mum, ran off with the kids to her sisters when things got too difficult for her at home, but my grandfather would go after them and drag them home after smashing all the windows.

Christmas's were very much celebrated and they would each receive a traditional stocking every year that contained an apple, an orange, (fruits not mobile phones or computers), nuts and a peg doll.

Mum was an intelligent child she passed what was called the eleven plus, which got her a place at the local grammar school, rather than the comprehensive school. This was mums opportunity to better herself and the start of what might have been a successful career. However, at this time her mother left her father and went to live with and married a man she had been working for as a housekeeper, who as the story was told by some would not take on the children, and by others that my Gran left the children behind so that my grandfather would not come chasing after her. By the time I was born Grandma had returned to my Grandfather, after my Grandmothers second husband had passed away.

After this breakup mum being the eldest daughter had to leave the Grammar school and take on the role of mother to the three younger children, her older brothers were soon away to do their National Service. She was thirteen at the time and was a mother to her siblings long before she was ever a mother to us. It was a difficult role for such a young child.   Granddad was not the easiest man to be around. He would come in and demand that his dinner be ready and put on the table. It didn't matter that mum may have been up on ladders cleaning the large Victorian windows or tending to the younger children at the time. He would demand she stop what she was doing and fetch him his grub that would be kept warm for his arrival home from the pit or the pub on the hob on the fire. On one occasion mum refused and so he fiercely threw the plate of dinner across the room, the food flying over the newly swept and polished floor. Mum in some respects became her father's wife and despite his volatile temper her main priority was protecting the younger children.

At eighteen, when her sister was old enough to look after the two younger children she went on an adventure to Blackpool and became a chambermaid in a quality hotel. She would often tell the story of how one of the rich ladies a guest at the hotel gave her a bottle of Channel perfume. I can remember her showing me this when I was a child, she had kept it and had only used it on very special occasions. I can recall one occasion when she dabbed some of this sweet smelling perfume behind my ears, as I watched in awe at her applying her makeup. I felt very grown up and special to be wearing the rich ladies perfume.   Eventually mum gave me this perfume and I took a liking to this fresh smell. Channel perfume at the time was only for the very rich and certainly not affordable for the working class girl my mum was.

In later years Mum would talk to me about how she always felt guilty about leaving her younger siblings behind. She always remained close to them in future years, and was the mother hen for most of her life to her younger siblings. In fact if my aunty Ann the youngest daughter had troubles, it would always be my mum she turned to rather than her own mum. I can remember many times in my own childhood when Aunty Ann came to live with us and she became almost like my older sister, sharing my room where we would often giggle way into the night, much to my parent's frustration. As a teenager I can recall going to dances with her, coming home tipsy and cooking pop corn in a pan trying not to wake up the whole household. Mum's youngest brother David tragically died in his fifties to a brain tumour and mum always said it was like losing a son rather than a brother. It broke her heart. Aunty Ann died with my mother by her side in hospital when she was 60 of COPD after being a heavy smoker for most of her life. For my mum she had lost two of her children, the children she raised.

On returning to Easington from her adventures mum found that her mum had returned to my Grandddad, so all was back to normal. She got herself a job at the local telephone exchange as an operator and it was then she met and married the local bad boy. Her parents particularly my grandad was not happy about this relationship, he refused to attend the wedding although I do believe he did turn up at the very last minute.

The beginning of my life was a sad one with my mum and myself being on the receiving end of severe domestic abuse on a regular basis from my violent father. I don't remember him at all as my mum managed to escape from him when I was still a baby. She had been to the local priest and asked about a divorce on several occasions to be told that she had married for better or worse. As determined as she was she eventually convinced the priest to change his mind. A letter was written to the cardinal or some higher being and she was allowed to divorce but told she must never marry again. She did. It was from this day forth my mum stopped being a practicing catholic.

She moved to Leicester to stay with her cousin Uncle Frank and his wife, Aunty Freda who were to always be a huge part of our family life. Mum felt that she had to get as far away as possible from her husband to feel safe. She had on one occasion left him prior to this, she had gone back to her parents house, but he had turned up at the door had a row with my grandfather and as the story is told knocked all his teeth out. Mum was determined not to have a life like her own mother so made the brave decision to move as far away as possible so that he would not find us. In those days there were very few if any single parents and those that were would be stigmatised, this demonstrates the strength and resilience that mum had who was still a young girl herself.

Stories I was later to learn in my own life were that my biological father would hold me by my feet over the stair banister threatening to drop me on my head to torment my mum. Apparently he would also regularly spit in my face, if he was angry with mum. This must have been so painful for her to see and knowing my mum she would have drawn his anger towards herself to protect her little one. This must have been very frightening for a baby too, who came into this world with her only needs to be born into a loving warm and kind family. Studies show that a baby is only born with two 'fears.' A fear of falling and a fear of loud noises, I was exposed to both at a very early age.

Alongside this I witnessed at a time when I was pre-verbal my mum being battered and bruised and would have felt her pain as strongly as she felt it. Most researchers in the field of psychology agree that the environment that a child is born into is of key importance to the child's development and psychological wellbeing.

The abuse I was part of, witnessed and experienced was infantile trauma creating unconscious, buried memories and emotions emerged in panic and anxiety at a time when I had no words to express how I was feeling. My poor mum would have struggled to maintain her own fear and anxiety let alone that of a dependent child. I experienced terror at a very early age which according to theory creates an 'annihilation anxiety' which persists throughout the person's life. Annihilation is indeed intensely painful for me, and for most of my life I have been in survival mode trying to prevent real or imagined situations whereby I might be annihilated. This without a doubt have been the cause of my reactive behaviours and strong painful emotions over the years.

As you will read further in this book I was most definitely annihilated by my brothers throughout our adult lives and at the end of my mother's life which explains the deep and unmanageable pain that I experienced each time this happened. Pain which my family failed to understand, pain that because this happened at the pre verbal stage of development I was unable to articulate coherently. I developed a fear of annihilation because for me it sent me straight back to that infantile trauma, opened up those early wounds and sent me right back to that baby that lived in terror. As you will see in the letters in the back of this book I tried chaotically to tell my family this but I did not have the language to explain it at the time, and even if I had we did not have a shared language for them to understand or indeed a shared experience and I have no doubt they would have laughed it off as psycho-babble.

People only try to understand if they have a genuine interest in you and I don't believe my brothers did when reaching adulthood. They were too enveloped within their own pain and anger of never being told the 'family secret' that only Mum, Dad and I knew. In, I guess their own painful feelings of annihilation, of not being included which possibly led to their own unconscious behaviours of exclusion of me.

To explain this psychological process to mum would have just filled her with guilt, she would have internalised it as her fault and I would never have wanted that. It was not her fault there was only one person at fault here and that was the man who could not keep his sadistic hands to himself. I am fully aware of how easy it is to become prey to a man who is violent, but that is another story for another day.

I shall be cool

CHILDRENS BOOKS by Linda Mather

A fairy tale for children between the ages of three and seven, or for all those that still
believe in the magic of Christmas.
Teaches children the importance of loneliness, sharing and friendships

Megan hates history, until she discovers the mystery behind Grandpa's chair. She sits
on it and finds herself in the middle of the Coventry blitz. For ages seven to fourteen.
Written with my beautiful Granddaughter Charlotte
Teaches children about history and the importance of knowing our history

I shall be cool

Crystal Magic

Written in collaboration with my beautiful Granddaughter, Emily   A superhero who is determined to find out who is playing tricks on the local community.
Teaches children about bulling and why some children bully

Friendships in the Rainforest

Written in collaboration with my beautiful Granddaughters, Scarlet, Lacey and Farron. A beautiful story of love, friendship and loyalty
Teaches children about empathy and love

SELF HELP BOOKS by Linda Mather

> For everyone's Emotional Development

> For people suffering with Depression

> For people with Substance Misuse problems

For
Anxiety Management

Anxiety Management for
children

Fun but informative book on
raising teenagers

Understanding a self
absorbed parent

I shall be cool

COUNSELLING TEXT BOOKS

An Introduction to counselling skills and theory

Training Manual for Certificate to Diploma in therapeutic counselling

I shall be cool

COMING SOON!

Available on Amazon October 2021

I shall be cool

I would love to hear your feedback please leave a review on Amazon UK

Or email me on

Bluebird.cptc@outlook.com